Crosscurrents / MODERN CRITIQUES

Harry T. Moore, *General Editor*

The Novels of
DORIS LESSING

Paul Schlueter

WITH A PREFACE BY

Harry T. Moore

SOUTHERN ILLINOIS UNIVERSITY PRESS
Carbondale and Edwardsville

FEFFER & SIMONS, INC.
London and Amsterdam

To

Samuel Holt Monk—
Distinguished Scholar
Respected Teacher
Esteemed Friend

Library of Congress Cataloging in Publication Data
Schlueter, Paul, 1933–
    The novels of Doris Lessing.
    (Crosscurrents/Modern critiques)
    Bibliography: p.
    1. Lessing, Doris May, 1919–
PR6023.E833Z88   823'.9'14   72–10281
ISBN 0–8093–0612–3

Contents

▼

Preface

Some years ago Paul Schlueter was a student in a course I taught in the contemporary British novel. One of our text-books, then too recent to be a paperback, was Doris Lessing's The Golden Notebook which, in a New Republic review, Irving Howe had greeted as the finest novel in English since the Second World War. Paul Schlueter manifested an interest in Doris Lessing and began writing about her. In 1965, Charles Shapiro brought out one of the most successful books in the Crosscurrents/Modern Critiques series, Contemporary British Novelists, and this volume contained an essay on Doris Lessing by Paul Schlueter. Then, in 1968, as part of his work toward a doctor of philosophy degree, he wrote a dissertation on Mrs. Lessing. In 1971, he organized a discussion group devoted to that author at the Chicago meetings of the Modern Language Association. The papers read on this occasion have been published by the University of Evansville as The Fiction of Doris Lessing, edited by Paul Schlueter.

In drawing upon the material for the present book from his dissertation, Dr. Schlueter has pointed out that in the latter he had "omitted as many pedantic touches as possible"; and now he has completely reshaped the material for the present volume. Doris Lessing is an author of great complexity, and this study provides us with a thorough analysis of every part of her fiction, which for the most part has two geographical settings, Africa and England. The stories are usually seen from a woman's point of view—in the old days we spoke of "feminism."

Doris Lessing's protagonists, whether the Martha Quest of the five novels in which she is dominant, or the Anna Freeman Wulf of The Golden Notebook, are representative of all that is considered avant-garde. They live through a great range of modern experience, of which Dr. Schlueter's investigation is clarifying and valuable.

Doris Lessing is certainly one of the most important postwar novelists, and Auberon Waugh's recent dismissal of her as "a rather silly woman who is led to suppose that this is the correct way to write" can itself be dismissed as silly in the face of Doris Lessing's achievement. This achievement is carefully measured by Dr. Schlueter, who doesn't fail to notice that, like all writers, Mrs. Lessing has her weaknesses, as exemplified in his discussion of Retreat to Innocence (1956). Doris Lessing herself isn't too fond of that particular book, which she now regards as "good material wasted." It is one of the noteworthy features of the present study of her work that Dr. Schlueter was in touch with Mrs. Lessing and thereby was enabled to add some material of the kind not often discovered in critical studies.

There are various examples of the latter in preparation and, as Dr. Schlueter notes, a number of university dissertations are now being written about Doris Lessing, who had been somewhat neglected by American academicians in the recent past. Dr. Schlueter's book is a pioneering work, but it is critically so thorough and expert that it should last for a long time.

HARRY T. MOORE

Southern Illinois University
September 21, 1972

Acknowledgments

There had been virtually nothing written about Doris Lessing's fiction when I first started working in earnest on it, both in preparation for my earlier essay (cited in the Bibliography) and for this book. In the past several years, however, interest in Lessing has reached sometimes fanatical proportions, and a number of studies have now been written or are in progress about Lessing, elucidating in greater and greater detail the subtleties of her work. Hence it is all the more important, I feel, that credit should be given to those others who wrote seriously about her work prior to today's bandwagon. I think especially of John (Alfred) A. Carey, who wrote the first doctoral study of Lessing; to James Gindin, for his valuable essay from over a decade ago; to Frederick P. W. McDowell, for his continued interest in and examination of Lessing's fiction; to two more recent scholars of her work, Diane Smith and Lois Marchino; and to Harry T. Moore, who first introduced me to Lessing's work. And profound thanks must also go to Doris Lessing herself, for occasional correspondence over several years in which incisive comments were offered to help make this study what it is. And to the participants in the first seminar on Lessing, held at the Modern Language Association's annual convention in December 1971, many thanks as well for the excitement of being able to share ideas about a woman increasingly recognized as a pivotal, indeed great, writer.

I wish to acknowledge with thanks permissions granted by various copyright holders and publishers—and especially Doris Lessing herself—to quote from the following works by Lessing and other authors cited in the text:

The Grass Is Singing by Doris Lessing. Copyright © 1950 by Doris Lessing. Reprinted by permission of Thomas Y. Crowell Company, Inc., and Curtis Brown Ltd.

Children of Violence, Volumes 1 and 2, by Doris Lessing. Copyright © 1952, 1954, 1964 by Doris Lessing. Reprinted by permission of Simon and Schuster, Inc., and Curtis Brown Ltd.

Children of Violence, Volumes 3 and 4, by Doris Lessing. Copyright © 1970 by Doris Lessing. Reprinted by permission of Simon and Schuster, Inc., and Curtis Brown Ltd.

Children of Violence, Volume 5, by Doris Lessing. Copyright © 1969 by Doris Lessing Productions Ltd. Reprinted by permission of Alfred A. Knopf, Inc., and Curtis Brown Ltd.

The Golden Notebook, by Doris Lessing. Copyright © 1962 by Doris Lessing. Reprinted by permission of Simon and Schuster, Inc., and Curtis Brown Ltd.

Interview with Doris Lessing, from *Counterpoint* by Roy Newquist. Copyright 1964 by Rand McNally & Co. Reprinted by permission of Rand McNally & Co.

"The Small Personal Voice" by Doris Lessing, from *Declaration,* ed. Tom Maschler. Published 1957 by MacGibbon and Kee. Reprinted by permission of Curtis Brown Ltd.

Going Home by Doris Lessing. Copyright © 1968 by Doris Lessing. Reprinted by permission of Curtis Brown Ltd.

Each His Own Wilderness by Doris Lessing. Copyright © 1959 by Doris Lessing. Reprinted by permission of Doris Lessing.

D. H. Lawrence, by R. P. Draper. Copyright © 1964 by Twayne Publishers, Inc. Reprinted by permission of Twayne Publishers, Inc.

Lines from "The Waste Land" (Part 5, lines 385–400) in *Collected Poems 1909–1962* by T. S. Eliot, copyright, 1936, by Harcourt Brace Jovanovich, Inc.; copyright © 1963, 1964, by T. S. Eliot. Reprinted by permission of Harcourt Brace Jovanovich, Inc., and Faber and Faber Ltd.

PAUL SCHLUETER

University of Evansville

May 1972

The Novels of Doris Lessing

1

Doris Lessing in Perspective

The pressures of our time frequently force upon sensitive people a greater awareness not only of the era itself but also of the individual in that era. In particular, such an awareness frequently takes the form of an analysis either of the complicated and bewildered individual in the world, or of the manner in which that individual relates to other human beings. Such "personal relations," as they have been called by Irving Howe [1] (with an awareness of the irony of the term), are "the very substance and sufficient end of our existence" and a "bulwark against the nihilist void, an ideology of privacy to replace the lapsed ideologies of public action." Of the multitude of novels written in our generation attempting to delve into the possibilities of "personal relations," many, as Howe comments, "suffer from a narrowness of perspective that approaches claustrophobia"; an extremely small handful of such novels, however, have not only avoided the limitations of the genre (e.g., perspective, tone), but have interwoven the intellectual sharpness and analytical acuteness typically associated with such novels with the critical detachment and objectivity more often associated with such genres as the sociological or documentary novel. Of the small handful of writers producing such books, few if any have probed more deeply into the question of what it means to be a woman in today's complex society— especially a woman involved with politics, with writing, with love and sex—than Doris Lessing, whose novels and stories present some of the finest contemporary expressions of the "lostness" and simultaneous self-awareness found in the sensitive person today.

Mrs. Lessing's vision, however, is not a complete negation of the possibility of self-knowledge or of meaningful existence. More than most of the writers concerned with the emancipated woman in the complex modern world—Mary McCarthy and Simone de Beauvoir readily come to mind —Mrs. Lessing is not content merely to bemoan the pressures of the world that can affect a woman's personal evaluation of herself, nor to describe as completely sterile whatever "personal relations" she may have. Rather, Mrs. Lessing, in all her fiction but especially in *The Golden Notebook* (1962), clearly advocates a personal commitment on the part of the individual which will enable that individual to relate meaningfully to others and to the world. And although this commitment can take various forms for various humans, it frequently becomes an allegiance to or enthusiasm for the struggles for racial freedom and integrity; political, usually Communist, affiliation and activity; love and/or marriage; and, ultimately the most important of all, the creative act of reading and writing as means of achieving the most lasting and significant commitment of all, commitment to personal freedom.

But although Doris Lessing has produced novels and short stories, drama, autobiography, social and personal essays, and even a thin volume of verse, with most of these volumes receiving warm praise from both popular and serious critics, she has yet to become more than merely a moderately familiar name in modern British literature to many American readers. Moreover, one of her books—*The Golden Notebook*—has impressed more than one critic as a masterpiece of its kind, leading to such extravagant acclaim as the statement by the critic for the London *Sunday Times* who found Mrs. Lessing "not only the best woman novelist we have, but one of the most serious, intelligent and honest writers of the whole post-war generation." [2] While critics on this side of the Atlantic have been only slightly less enthusiastic in their reception of this and other books, Mrs. Lessing has still to make a significant impact on either chroniclers of the modern novel [3] or on a widespread popular or educated audience. Furthermore, extended discussion of her work in more specialized form, in dissertations or critical essays, is slight: aside from my earlier essay [4] there have been only a relatively small handful of detailed assessments.[5] Hence it is all the more important for a study of Mrs. Lessing's major longer fiction to include some biographical data if Mrs. Lessing's life and career are to be seen in perspective. For she has maintained with rigorous singleness of vision emphases on themes which, while certainly not unique to her alone, are presented with such artistic integrity and forcefulness as to warrant the full measure of the enthusiastic critical comments she has thus far received. Because of the drastically limited amount of commonly-known information about her life and work, however, it is necessary to provide, in brief fashion, basic biographical facts (drawn from a variety of sources),[6] and brief discussions of plot.

Doris May Lessing was born in Kermanshah, Persia, on October 22, 1919. Her father, Alfred Cook Tayler, before the war had been an English bank clerk; during the war he served as both enlisted man and officer in the French campaign. Seriously wounded prior to the battle of Passchendaele, he was hospitalized, had to have a leg amputated, and shortly thereafter married his nurse. Finding life difficult in England, he emigrated to Persia to work in banking. In 1925 he left Persia for Southern Rhodesia, to an area a hundred miles west of Mozambique, where he began farming. Much of Doris's youth was spent in the hills and plains in the area of her father's farm, though she attended a convent school until she was fourteen; since her nearest neighbors while on the farm were several miles away, she and others in the same situation were continually eager to get away from such an isolated setting. But eye trouble cut her formal schooling short, forcing her to rely upon her own extensive reading in the major nineteenth-century Russian, French, and English novelists.

In 1938 she moved to Salisbury both to work in an office and to begin writing. The following year she married Frank

Charles Wisdom, giving birth to a son and a daughter before the marriage ended in divorce in 1943. Two years later she married Gottfried Lessing, giving birth to a son before this marriage also ended in divorce in 1949. The same year she left Southern Rhodesia for England with her younger son and the manuscript of her first book, a novel based on her African life, *The Grass Is Singing*. She at first took a job in an office in London, but quit when her novel was published the following year.

That Doris Lessing should have identified herself with the Communist party in Great Britain is itself not surprising, for the C.P.G.B. had for a number of years appealed more strongly to the intellectuals and writers of England than its counterpart in, say, the United States. Many British intellectuals, for instance, had fought for the Republican cause during the Spanish civil war, and half of the Britons killed in the war had been Communists. But there was also a strong spirit of individualism in the C.P.G.B., a spirit Doris Lessing fully shared. In 1956, for instance, a short-lived unofficial Communist periodical dedicated to a greater variety of opinion was published, with Mrs. Lessing as one of its chief contributors. When the party continued repeating the Stalinist line and defending Soviet intervention after the Hungarian Revolt in October 1956, Mrs. Lessing and many others left the party for good, creating a crisis in the party and a drastic, continued loss of members. The impassioned dedication to social justice felt by Mrs. Lessing and others is repeatedly seen in her novels, and communism in particular serves as the means by which this justice can be effected, although, as the chronological analyses of the novels comprising the bulk of this study will show, communism as a cause becomes less and less tenable a means of creating a desirable society. For example, the novel published just prior to the Hungarian Revolt, *Retreat to Innocence*, reflects the peak of enthusiasm for communism found in her books, while *The Golden Notebook*, published in 1962, shows a consistent lack of faith in communism as a commitment.[7]

The years since Mrs. Lessing's arrival in England have

Doris Lessing in Perspective   5

resulted in a steady stream of books, with no sign at the present of any diminution of output or talent. Included in the many volumes are collections of short stories (*This Was the Old Chief's Country*, 1951; *The Habit of Loving*, 1957; *A Man and Two Women*, 1963; and *African Stories*, 1964); the five novels in the *Children of Violence* series (*Martha Quest*, 1952; *A Proper Marriage*, 1954; *A Ripple from the Storm*, 1958; *Landlocked*, 1965; and *The Four-Gated City*, 1969); several novelettes and other novels (*The Grass Is Singing*, 1950; *Five*, 1953; *Retreat to Innocence*, 1956; *The Golden Notebook*, 1962; *Briefing for a Descent into Hell*, 1971); volumes of social or autobiographical commentary (*Going Home*, 1957; *In Pursuit of the English*, 1960; *Particularly Cats*, 1967), several plays (*Each His Own Wilderness*, 1959; *Play with a Tiger*, 1962); and a volume of verse (*Fourteen Poems*, 1959). She has had numerous essays and articles published, as well as two other plays produced but not published.[8] As mentioned above, she shows no sign at present of diminishing the flow of writing; indeed, since she is at this writing only in her early fifties, she can reasonably be expected to continue her seemingly inexhaustible exploration of certain basic themes for some years to come.

But if quantity of production were Doris Lessing's chief or even her only literary attribute, there would be little intrinsic reason to explore her major novels in depth, for there are most assuredly other, more prolific writers more readily accessible to analysis and more easily seen in perspective. It is my thesis, therefore, that Mrs. Lessing has something exceedingly significant to say about themes which have concerned many less talented writers of our day: the appeal of communism to the liberals of the late 1930s and early 1940s; the black-white situation in British colonial Africa; the role of the "free" woman in an essentially masculine world, and the manifestations, particularly sexual, of that woman's keen self-analysis; and the function of writing as a means of achieving therapeutic identity, even equilibrium, in a chaotic universe. This is not to suggest that she emphasizes all these themes uniformly in her several novels, nor even that she consistently handles them all well, anymore than she excels in creating different women in each novel, since Mrs. Lessing's heroines, whatever their names or circumstances, seem to share certain basic traits; but she does make such ideas as the inefficacy of communism or the struggle for racial justice vivid enough so that they become the dominant concern in the discussions of the various novels. There is, indeed, a certain kind of progression in her handling of these themes, as will be suggested by comparative comments in each chapter. But regardless of the particular idea being discussed, all are made most viable and pertinent to our day in Mrs. Lessing's foremost novel, *The Golden Notebook*. Hence all succeeding remarks about the other novels should be considered as preliminary comments to the novel which seems to me to state Mrs. Lessing's position regarding communism, race, love, and freedom, with greatest vigor and precision.

2

The Grass Is Singing

In 1949, Doris Lessing arrived in London with her small
son and the manuscript of her first book, *The Grass Is Singing*. Nearly penniless, she had the unexpected pleasure of
having the manuscript accepted within three days of its submission to a publisher. The book was overwhelmingly well
received by both the critics and the public, and it went
through seven reprintings within five months.[1] The book
takes its title from part 5 of T. S. Eliot's *The Waste Land*:

> In this decayed hole among the mountains
> In the faint moonlight, the grass is singing
> Over the tumbled graves, about the chapel
> There is the empty chapel, only the wind's home.
> It has no windows, and the door swings,
> Dry bones can harm no one.
> Only a cock stood on the rooftree
> Co co rico co co rico
> In a flash of lightning. Then a damp gust
> Bringing rain
>
> Ganga was sunken, and the limp leaves
> Waited for rain, while the black clouds
> Gathered far distant, over Himavent.
> The jungle crouched, humped in silence.
> Then spoke the thunder
>
> [5.385–400]

As will be seen later, there are explicit parallels between
this passage and Mrs. Lessing's novel.

Most of Doris Lessing's fiction, beginning with *The Grass Is Singing* and continuing through the several parts of the *Children of Violence* series and *The Golden Notebook*, is either set in Africa or looks back to an African setting. Only in her fourth novel, *Retreat to Innocence*, a minor work, and in the final Martha Quest novel is the plot free of direct involvement in African matters, and the characters without an African background. Hence in this first novel, so overwhelmingly concerned with black-white tensions in colonial Africa, we are introduced to what remains a pervasive theme. Mrs. Lessing has repeatedly expressed her feelings regarding her African upbringing and the feelings of racial injustice saturating both Southern Rhodesia and South Africa, nations that have subsequently placed her on their lists of "prohibited aliens" (despite her many years of residence in Southern Rhodesia), following a return trip to Africa in 1956.[2] She has described her youth as being a "member of the white minority, pitted against a black majority that was abominably treated and still is. . . . It was all grossly unfair, and it's only part of a larger picture of inequity."[3] Her outspoken attitude toward the "colour bar" has led her to state that "one cannot write truthfully about Africa without describing it," and that

> if one has been at great pains to choose a theme which is more general, people are so struck by the enormity and ugliness of the colour prejudices which must be shown in it that what one has tried to say gets lost.[4]

But as an enlightened expatriate from colonial Africa, Mrs. Lessing is better able to see clearly the inevitable and necessary social change in racial relationships than are those who are still part of the *apartheid* society. She has said, for instance, that she longs

> for the moment when the Africans can free themselves and can express themselves in new forms, new ways of living; they are an original and vital people simply because they have been forced to take the jump from tribalism to industrial living in one generation.[5]

She says, moreover, that "because she was brought up in it, she has a responsibility" in the subject.[6] Thus the emphasis given to it in her first novel is both justified and expected.

The plot of *The Grass Is Singing* is itself relatively simple and uncomplicated. We are informed at the outset that Mary Turner, the wife of a farmer, has been killed by a houseboy, that the murderer was caught, and that he confessed to the crime. After elaborately telling of the anguish, even emotional collapse, of the husband, Dick, Mrs. Lessing emphasizes the reactions of two other whites, Charlie Slatter, a neighbor, and Tony Marston, an idealistic twenty-year-old and recent immigrant from England who had been working on the Turner farm for only a short time. Following this initial chapter, Mrs. Lessing goes back to Mary Turner's childhood and tells of her gradual acceptance of an isolated, unmarried life, of her desperate acceptance of marriage at the age of thirty, of her subsequent adjustment to life on a desolate and unprofitable farm, her brutal treatment of natives, the complete mental and economic deterioration both she and her husband experience, the sale of the farm to Slatter (with Dick retained as manager and with Tony scheduled to step in as Charlie's representative when the Turners take a rest trip), and culminating with her murder. It is, in fact, a straightforward chronological plot, with the final chapter of such a sequence placed first in the narrative and with the rest of the book constituting an extended flashback.

At the heart of the book is the struggle the various whites have in refusing to accept the blacks as human—not as equals, but merely as human. To this end the various unwritten laws of colonial Africa that are frequently mentioned in the novel serve as convenient support for an arrogant kind of exclusivism. Referred to as an *esprit de corps* (pp. 11–12), these laws are invoked both for excessively cruel treatment of the blacks (p. 94), and for the necessity of whites maintaining a proper status in the colonies. Slatter, for instance,

was obeying the dictate of the first law of white South Africa, which is: "Thou shalt not let your fellow whites sink lower than a certain point; because, if you do, the nigger will see he is as good as you are." [P. 221]

So rigid are the laws regarding black-white contact, for instance, that the houseboy, Moses, cannot ride in the same car as the corpse of Mary Turner: "one could not put a black man close to a white woman, even though she were dead, and murdered by him" (pp. 28–29). Thus the black becomes the "constant, the invariable, the epitome of crime and violence" (p. 29); with the whites having behind them the police, the courts, the jails, all the natives can exert is patience (p. 148). Even the black policemen are not permitted to touch a white man in the pursuit of their duties (p. 13). As a whole, the whites "loathe [the natives] to the point of neurosis" (p. 92), and refer to them contemptuously as "animals" (p. 142) and "swine" (p. 69), among other terms.

So certain are the whites of the necessity and rightness of their treatment of the blacks that newcomers to the country are immediately made aware of the difference between, say, England and Southern Rhodesia (pp. 20–21). Tony Marston at first thought only in such abstractions (p. 226), holding "the conventionally 'progressive' ideas about the colour bar, the superficial progressiveness of the idealist that seldom survives a conflict with self-interest" (p. 226). Hence he frequently started discussions with established white settlers on miscegenation, only to have his "progressiveness" "deliciously flattered by . . . evidence of white ruling-class hypocrisy" (p. 230). Following Mary's murder, he

would do his best to forget the knowledge, for to live with the colour bar in all its nuances and implications means closing one's mind to many things, if one intends to remain an accepted member of society. [P. 30]

Tony soon realizes that "Moses would be hanged in any case," for "he had committed a murder, that fact remained. Did he intend to go on fighting in the dark for the sake of a principle? And if so, which principle?" (p. 31). It is thus no surprise that Marston is a broken man. Although we are not told what Marston's behavior henceforth is like, we can predict fairly safely, on the basis of Mrs. Lessing's discussions in Africa on her return visit, what is likely to occur.

> Time and again it was said to me, either jubilantly or with regret, "If you want to see the natives badly treated, then you should see the people just out from Britain: they are worse than anyone, much worse than the old Rhodesians." And "We thought that a big influx of immigrants from Britain would strengthen liberal opinion, but not a bit of it." [7]

Thus Marston's understanding of the situation is for him to see

> "white civilization" fighting to defend itself . . . implicit in the attitude of Charlie Slatter and the Sergeant, "white civilization" which will never, never admit that a white person, and most particularly, a white woman, can have a human relationship, whether for good or for evil, with a black person. For once it admits that, it crashes, and nothing can save it. [P. 30]

Tony, in short, becomes much like most others of the white minority in his attitudes toward the natives.

But Mary, as a native Southern Rhodesian, has none of this analytic perspective on the racial problem. Before she came to Dick Turner's farm, she had never had any direct contact with natives, but had developed a "code" of behavior toward them just as the natives had toward her. This "code," consisting of "politeness not to look a superior in the face" (p. 82), Mary takes to be merely further indication of the natives' "shifty and dishonest nature." She of course had known previously that the natives were getting "cheeky" (p. 42), but since this was at the time "outside her orbit," it meant nothing. Now, though, she is outraged at the too-casual behavior of a native (p. 69); she is intent on teaching the natives about "the dignity of work, which is a doctrine bred into the bones of every white South African" (p. 140); and she hates their physical vitality and suggestion of raw fertility and virility, as will be discussed in more detail below.

Although Mary can order Moses, she remains in fear of him from the outset of his stay in the house (pp. 174–75), and gradually but inexorably he becomes her master in ways she dare not admit consciously to herself. When she breaks down emotionally (p. 185), she is self-conscious at Moses' presence, and before long realizes that "there was now a new relation between them."

> She felt helplessly in his power. Yet there was no reason why she should. Never ceasing for one moment to be conscious of his presence about the house, or standing silently at the back against the wall in the sun, her feeling was one of a strong and irrational fear, a deep uneasiness, and even—though this she did not know, would have died rather than acknowledge—of some dark attraction. It was as though the act of weeping before him had been an act of resignation of her authority; and he had refused to hand it back. Several times the quick rebukes had come to her lips, and she had seen him look at her deliberately, not accepting it, but challenging her. Only once, when he had really forgotten to do something and was in the wrong, had he worn his old attitude of black submissiveness. Then he accepted, because he was at fault. And now she began to avoid him. . . . And she was held in balance, not knowing what this new tension was that she could not break down. [Pp. 190–91]

This new relationship does not take the form of overt disrespect. He does call her "madame" instead of the usual "missus," as most blacks did to their white overlords (p. 192), but "although he was never disrespectful, he forced her, now to treat him as a human being" (p. 192). He even dares to touch her, to help her to lie down to sleep.

> He put out his hand reluctantly, loathe to touch her, the sacrosanct white woman, and pushed her by the shoulder; she felt herself gently propelled across the room towards the bedroom. It was like a nightmare where one is

powerless against horror: the touch of this black man's hand on her shoulder filled her with nausea; she had never, not once in her whole life, touched the flesh of a native. [P. 186]

But as previously noted, Mary's relationship changes, and although nothing resembling or suggesting an immoral liaison occurs, she does accept his touch. In fact, it is Tony's observing Moses put Mary's dress on her and button it up that leads to the sense of rejection that Moses feels and to the subsequent murder.

Mrs. Lessing, in describing her trip back to Southern Rhodesia, indicates that the subject of black-white contact always comes up when racial equality is discussed, that it is the "stock South African conversation." [8] So artificial is the gulf between the whites and the blacks in this novel that the whites resent and attempt to help those whites who degenerate to the level of the blacks, just as they resent and attempt to hinder those blacks who attempt to rise to the level of the whites. But since such natives as the houseboy, Moses, gain an advantage over their white overlords as the whites deteriorate, the whites find it more and more difficult to maintain the fiction of white supremacy.

Mary, for example, had ruthlessly and brutally whipped Moses across his face when he was working in the fields. When Mary first came to the farm, "she could not understand any white person feeling anything personal about a native" (p. 78); but as Moses continues to influence and dominate her, she is said to be

beyond reflecting that her anger, her hysteria, was over nothing, nothing that she could explain. What had happened was that the formal pattern of black-and-white, mistress-and-servant, had been broken by the personal relation; and when a white man in Africa by accident looks into the eyes of a native and sees the human being (which it is his chief preoccupation to avoid), his sense of guilt, which he denies, fumes up in resentment and he brings down the whip. [Pp. 177-78]

There is thereafter the "new relation between them" mentioned above; the power this new relationship reflects becomes increasingly malevolent, and repeatedly in the final pages of the novel, Moses' very presence in the house leads Charlie, Dick, and especially Tony to express fear of Moses' arrogant behavior and the possibility of violence occurring. Moses knows that Tony is the only white with whom he must contend, for he knows Dick had been defeated long before. Rather than to escape, though, Moses ponders the house and Mary's body:

> And this was his final moment of triumph, a moment so perfect and complete that it took the urgency from thoughts of escape, leaving him indifferent. . . . Though what thoughts of regret, or pity, or perhaps even wounded human affection were compounded with the satisfaction of his completed revenge, it is impossible to say. [Pp. 255–56]

Thus although Moses achieves his revenge, he knows also the impossibility of escape. Hence Mary's lapse in discipline over a native becomes, for the whites remaining in power, merely one more practical example to support the white-supremacist tenet that the blacks are not fit to be treated as humans, since the "black man . . . will thieve, rape, murder, if given half a chance" (p. 29). And once again Mary's initial fear of "personal relations" with the natives becomes the guiding principle for other white women in Southern Rhodesia, with Mary's death only serving to document the impossibility of such relationships being started or maintained to the advantage of the whites.

But Mary's initial hesitation in establishing personal relationships with the natives is not the only way in which she is reluctant to enter fully into life and its problems. Throughout her life Mary had been isolated, both in fact and in feeling, and this isolation had created in her a feeling of noninvolvement in the lives and feelings of others that she calls "freedom." This "freedom," however, is not at all akin to the sense in which this term is used by the female protagonists of Mrs. Lessing's later fiction, for the "freedom" Mary Turner claims for herself is considerably less viable and carefully reasoned than it is for Mrs. Lessing's later central characters. Her real freedom, she believes, comes only after her parents' death, for then she is unhindered from her personal pursuit, although even then her innate fear of involvement can be seen; for although she is "free," she is not free at this time to enter into others' lives. Even after her marriage, she still attempts to emulate the vague feminism she inherited from her mother.

> The women who marry men like Dick learn sooner or later that there are two things they can do: they can drive themselves mad, tear themselves to pieces in storms of futile anger and rebellion; or they can hold themselves tight and go bitter. Mary, with the memory of her own mother recurring more and more frequently, like an older, sardonic double of herself walking beside her, followed the course her upbringing made inevitable. [P. 110]

The irony of Mary's situation, as the preceding quotation suggests, is that she begins her exile on the farm completely embittered, only in the last years before her death rebelling against both her husband and her class and race, and finally being torn apart herself as a consequence of her unwise behavior.

Mary's unwillingness to enter fully into the realm of the personal is especially clear in her attitude toward and reactions against sexuality. Although "sentimental" at weddings, she throughout her life feels a "profound distaste for sex. . . . there had been little privacy in her home and there were things she did not care to remember; she had taken good care to forget them years ago" (p. 46). Thus she prefers being treated "like a good pal, with none of this silly sex business," when she dates (p. 47). When she does marry Dick, she feels, following her deflowering on the wedding night, that

> It was not so bad, . . . when it was all over: not as bad as *that*. It meant nothing to her, nothing at all. Expecting outrage and imposition, she was relieved to find she

felt nothing. She was able maternally to bestow the gift of herself on this humble stranger, and remain untouched. Women have an extraordinary ability to withdraw from the sexual relationship, to immunize themselves against it, in such a way that their men can be left feeling let down and insulted without having anything tangible to complain of. Mary did not have to learn this, because it was natural to her, and because she had expected nothing in the first place. [Pp. 66–67]

But although Mary finds the idea of normal sexual relations with Dick repulsive, both her subconscious, expressed through dreams, and her psychotic state toward the end of her life demonstrate the extent to which an abnormal or unusual sexual manifestation is desired.

Like others of Mrs. Lessing's protagonists, Mary too has frequent nightmares (e.g., pp. 58–59, 192, 199–201, 204, 206–7, 238, 241–43, 252); although earlier in life she had occasionally had dreams filled with wishful imaginings (e.g., pp. 120, 125, 159), the nightmares increase in frequency and intensity as her psychosis grows. All too often these dreams are either explicitly or implicitly sexual in nature, as when she dreams of her father forcing her symbolically to perform fellatio (p. 200), or when Dick and her father merge in an obscene vision (p. 203). In her paranoid delirium, she believes that Tony has come to "save" her, and that he too is interested in her sexually (pp. 235–46). In her waking state, she is obsessed with the proximity of the houseboy to her bed, "with nothing but the thin brick wall separating them" (p. 197), and with his physique vividly before her (p. 198). Mary finds that "the thought of the African grew obsessive. It was a nightmare, the powerful black man always in the house with her, so that there was no escape from his presence. She was possessed by it" (p. 206). When Tony encounters Moses buttoning Mary's dress, she immediately thinks of the "code," of miscegenation, and frantically shouts, "They said I was not like that, not like that, not like that" (p. 232). When Charlie comes to the Turner house toward the end of the book, she dresses so seductively and coquettishly that even the hard-

ened, worldly-wise Slatter is bothered (pp. 217–19), particularly when she addresses Moses "with exactly the same flirta-
tious coyness with which she had spoken to himself" (p.
219).

The peculiarly obsessive state in which Mary finds herself in the novel takes several unusual turns. In common
with most other whites, she believes that the natives, if
left to their own discipline, would rape and murder and in
general operate by means of primitive emotions. Mary thoroughly examines Moses when she first meets him (p. 147),
only to have the situation reverse itself later when he looks
her over closely (pp. 204–5). Ironically, this initial encounter results from Mary's refusal to give Moses a drink of water (p. 146), only to have Moses tenderly offer her a glass
of water when she gets hysterical (p. 186). She obsessively
tries to clean a zinc-lined bathtub, "as if she were scrubbing
skin off a black face" (p. 82; cf. p. 88). Early in her stay on
the farm she fears the houseboy's touching her clothing
(p. 84), only to encourage this just before the murder
(p. 230). But most of all she hates the native women:

> She hated the exposed fleshiness of them, their soft
> brown bodies and soft bashful faces that were also in-
> solent and inquisitive. . . . She could not bear to see
> them sitting there on the grass, their legs tucked under
> them in that traditional timeless pose, peaceful and un-
> caring. . . . Above all, she hated the way they suckled
> their babies, with their breasts hanging down for every-
> one to see; there was something in their calm satisfied
> maternity that made her blood boil. "Their babies hang-
> ing on to them like leeches," she said to herself shudder-
> ing, for she thought with horror of suckling a child. The
> idea of a child's lips on her breasts made her feel quite
> sick. . . . She did not think of herself, but rather of these
> black women, as strange; they were alien and primitive
> creatures with ugly desires she could not bear to think
> about. [Pp. 115–16; cf. p. 134]

Her obsessions, indeed, become ironically the means of her
own destruction. For her hatred of the natives and unwillingness to enter fully into certain basic areas of life, sup-

ported as these obsessions are by her admirable use of reason (see, for example, her attempt by using logic to persuade the natives that they are wrong, p. 140), are doomed to failure. As her sense of defeat is inextricably intertwined with her madness and loss of will in the final pages of the novel, so her stoical acceptance of death (p. 249) becomes her only alternative form of action. And even this stoicism parallels a numbness felt much earlier (pp. 125–26), the "beginning of an inner disintegration."

The final day or two of her life reflect certain atmospheric qualities that make the epigraph from Eliot's *The Waste Land* particularly appropriate. Throughout her stay on the farm, Mary had been keenly aware of the oppressive sun and heat, but on the days in question the solar brilliance is especially noticeable, combined as it is with "an intimation of that terror which would later engulf her" (p. 237) and a feeling of "release and lighthearted joy" (p. 238). She realizes that rain is imminent—but only after her death (p. 250). As Moses approaches to kill her, "she heard the thunder growl and shake in the trees," and she sees Moses in the flash of lightning (p. 253). As she dies, Moses hears the rain falling on the corrugated steel roof (p. 254), reminding him of the blood on the piece of steel with which he had killed her; he washes off the blood, then throws it down as if to say that it makes little difference whether he is caught or not. As the thunder "speaks," the purifying rains suggest, as in Eliot's poem, the revitalization of the earth.

Compared to Mrs. Lessing's later novels, *The Grass Is Singing* seems relatively derivative, not only with the explicit parallel to the Eliot poem but also such possible and suggestive sources as *Macbeth* (in the frantic efforts of Mary Turner to clean the metal tub, as if she were washing herself of her own guilt, and in Moses' successful but meaningless washing of the knife after the murder), the French naturalists (since Mary's entire experience on the farm and with those with whom she comes in contact being explicitly based on heredity and environment), and, most important of all, D. H. Lawrence. It has been plausibly suggested that *The Grass Is Singing* reminds the reader of Lawrence's *Lady Chatterley's Lover*.

The Grass Is Singing is a study of the decay of a marriage between an ill-matched couple who live on a poverty-stricken, incompetently managed farm on the Rhodesian veld. The sexlessness of their marriage is a parallel to the impotence of Sir Clifford Chatterley, but it has its roots in poverty and deprivation rather than in industrialism and false "liberalism." The black houseboy who becomes the Mellors intruding on this relationship is ambiguously regarded by the white woman. He brings destruction instead of rebirth; and it is not destruction of a cleansing Lawrentian kind, but the violent culmination of a long, demoralizing process. Yet the peculiar compulsion which the houseboy exerts over the white woman is intensely Lawrentian; and the scene in which the woman accidentally comes upon him when he is washing himself is clearly derived from Lady Chatterley. The breaking of the "formal pattern of black-and-white, mistress-and-servant" by the "personal relation"—against all the racial instincts of the woman—is also reminiscent of the way in which Mellors, simply by being what he is, breaks through the class barrier which Connie instinctively raises between them.[9]

While perhaps making too much of certain obvious parallels, and clearly assuming too much in some particulars (for example, Moses does bring about a kind of rebirth and cleansing, as discussed above), it is certainly true that Lawrence, rather than, say, Virginia Woolf, who has also been cited as a possible influence on Mrs. Lessing,[10] is a tangible influence on this novel. Perhaps the finest example of such influence, however, comes not from *Lady Chatterley's Lover* but from *Women in Love*. As quoted above, Mary Turner finds the native women repulsively obvious in their sexual and maternal qualities, similar to the revulsion felt by Gerald Crich and Gudrun Brangwen in Lawrence's book at the sight of primitive carvings depicting a native woman in childbirth.[11] Again, though, citation of such parallels is not intended to prove direct influence so much as Mrs. Lessing's being "closer in spirit and method"[12] to Lawrence than one might otherwise have assumed.

Mrs. Lessing has said that the murder recounted in *The Grass Is Singing* is itself not based on a factual incident, though there was of course the inevitable gossip regarding native servants going beyond assumed propriety in their relations with white mistresses.[13] The book itself, Mrs. Lessing has also said, "could have been about white people anywhere south of the Zambezi, white people who were not up to what is expected of them in a society where there is very heavy competition from the black people coming up." [14] She describes the book as being a "very driven book, I mean, there isn't much 'hope' in it." She adds that there isn't any progress from Moses to a native leader mentioned in *The Golden Notebook*, Tom Mathlong: "forgive me, but why should there be?" [15] Similarly, there is no real parallel between Mary Turner and Mrs. Lessing's other female protagonists, all of whom do achieve a certain degree of "freedom" in their lives, and who explore meaningfully the various "commitments" open to them in the modern world. Mary Turner, by contrast, denies herself such commitments, thus making of her life a sterile, empty existence, symbolized not only by her childlessness but also by the wasteland in which she lives.[16]

As a novel, then, *The Grass Is Singing* is a mixture of rather ordinary technical accomplishments and subtle psychological explorations. The essential conflict between individuals and groups of individuals, for instance, rarely seems to rise above the usual black-white reasoning found in any racist setting; in the case of this novel, though, the blacks invariably seem more sinned against than sinning, uniformly reflect a stoical acceptance of the inevitable injustice and prejudice in their world, and revert to primitive violence only, as with Moses, when pushed beyond their level of tolerance. The blacks are also generally stereotyped, again evidently because of the rigidly stratified society they are in: they are faithful and hardworking under white supervision, doubtfully educable, and never to be trusted. But just as the foregoing reflects the attitude of the dominant white society in Southern Rhodesia, so the whites themselves seem two-dimensional and lacking in substance.

All, even the well-meaning newcomers from England, operate purely by emotional reactions to the natives, usually
seeing efforts to bridge the gulf between the races in the
predictably erotic terms found among, say, southern whites
in our country. For the society of which Mrs. Lessing is
writing is essentially a rural slave society, with masters and
servants clearly knowing their places and never upsetting
the racial *status quo.*

It is, rather, in the exploration of psychological conflicts
within individuals in the book where Mrs. Lessing's strength
lies, in both this early fictional effort and in her later, more
carefully worked out, novels. For instance, merely knowing
that Moses is the murderer says nothing about the forces at
work in and on him that lead him to commit murder. Mrs.
Lessing's inexorable chronicling of the injustices and humil-
iations and dehumanized treatments received by the natives
enables us to see the "why" behind the killing, just as her
persistent probing into Mary Turner's thinking and reactions enables us to see the unthinking mentality of an entire way of life laid bare. Even though the whites who survive Mary see her death as an example to support their blind
thinking about the blacks, to the reader the book takes on
more of an allegorical or mythical quality, on a very limited
scale, suggesting to us that such persistent refusal to accept
the blacks as fully human as we see in the novel only results
in genocide. While the whites may have the physical power
to force their advantage, the blacks have a decidedly moral
advantage over their white overlords.

Similarly, Mrs. Lessing's portrayal of Mary Turner, two-
dimensional as it may seem at times, warrants closer
examination because of the unique perspective Mrs. Lessing
brings to bear on the female psyche. Mary Turner is far
less complicated than Mrs. Lessing's protagonists in the
Children of Violence series and *The Golden Notebook,* but
she shares with them a persistent self-examination and analysis, an obsessive concern about female sexuality, self-conscious concern about "freedom" in an essentially masculine
world, and a slight awareness, abortive though it may seem
in comparison with the later novels, with the racial dichot-

omy existing in colonial Africa. As a first novel, the book certainly contains examples of thinking and technique that a more experienced writer, such as Mrs. Lessing herself in more recent years, would prefer to alter, but it is nonetheless a relatively distinguished first novel, particularly because it contains within itself the seeds of ideas explored more openly and fully in the series of novels about Martha Quest and in *The Golden Notebook*.

3

The *Children of Violence* Series

The continual interest among British writers of fiction for the series of interrelated novels in which the same individuals are followed from youth to maturity, and best illustrated earlier this century in Galsworthy's *Forsyte Saga*, has found many recent practitioners. C. P. Snow's now-completed series, *Strangers and Brothers*, Anthony Powell's *A Dance to the Music of Time*, Lawrence Durrell's *Alexandria Quartet*, and L. P. Hartley's *Eustace and Hilda* novels are some of the more distinguished contemporary examples of this literary form, usually thought of as more distinctively French or German than English. A series different from all these others in vitality and in psychological, political, and sexual profundity is Doris Lessing's five-part *Children of Violence* series. Mrs. Lessing has indicated that the series is "a study of the individual conscience in its relations with the collective," [1] a point, she says, missed by all the early critics of the series, but one increasingly obvious as the series has developed and as the character of the series' protagonist, Martha Quest, has deepened.[2] In the first volume, Martha Quest, aged fifteen, is eager to live and to break away from her confining home. Living on a genteel but far from wealthy farm on the veld, Martha, her domineering, self-righteous, hypocritical, and above all possessive mother, and her tired, well-meaning, and sickly father (along with a younger brother, Jonathan, mentioned only in passing) maintain a kind of peaceful coexistence until Martha decides to work in the city as a secretary after finishing high school instead of going into the university. She has read widely, and has become friends with the sons of a local merchant, Solly and Joss Cohen, who are an active part of her later life. She also learns the practical differences between her own status as a white and the status enjoyed by the natives. When she moves to Zambesia (i.e., Salisbury), she still has many bookish ideas about emancipation and maturing, and thus is easily shocked at the white power structure controlling the city. She subsequently becomes part of a "sports club," and begins to date—at first with Donovan Anderson, a mother's boy, talented amateur dress designer, and probable homosexual. Getting almost no food or sleep, Martha is caught up in the exhilarating life she has longed for. At the same time, she discovers a liberal, leftist clique through Joss Cohen's intervention. Her first sexual experiences come about when she daringly dates Adolph "Dolly" King, a Jewish drummer in the sports club orchestra. After this relationship ends, she meets Douglas Knowell, also nominally left-wing, and after great social pressure, agrees to marry him.

The second novel in the series shows Martha and Douglas as a socially active young couple, usually to be found at sundown (i.e., cocktail) parties with their many friends. When war is declared, Douglas and many of his contemporaries go off to war (although he is never an actual part of it, serving in an isolated part of the African continent), and Martha, discovering that she is pregnant (indeed, that she was pregnant when she got married), is primarily concerned with preparations for childbirth. The numerous RAF men now stationed near the city lead Martha and others in the left-wing organization to think more about the possibilities of advocating the end of the "colour bar" than the white Africans had previously, for the military, mostly from England, are far less concerned with the rigid racial categories of African (i.e., native), "Coloured" (i.e., mulatto), and white than are the whites controlling the economy of the city. The baby is finally born, and Martha increasingly takes part in political activities. Douglas, declared unfit for further service, returns and sets up a comfortable home in the suburbs for Martha and their daughter, Caroline. But Martha finds such a life increasingly out of touch with the realities of life, and she moreover finds her husband intolerable and dull. When he goes on a four-week business trip, she begins anew her political activism. Her parents in the meantime have moved to the city, with Mrs. Quest constantly interfering in her daughter's home. Mr. Quest, though, sees the basic problem that exists between Martha and Douglas, and advises her, since she is not in love, not to have any more children by him. When Douglas returns, he sees the changes that have taken place, especially the romantic and the political. As a conventional civil servant, he says he cannot allow her left-wing activities, and when Martha threatens to leave him and her daughter, he acts hysterically. She in turn asks Joss and Solly's cousin Jasmine for advice, and is told to leave her husband because of the imperative need for help in the political realm.

The gossip in Zambesia, early in the third volume, has Martha involved in an affair with William, an air force officer; Douglas's influence in getting William sent to another part of the world effectively finishes the minute amount of affection Martha has for her husband. Others from the air force base, though, are actively involved in the left-wing group, as are a few refugees from Europe. One of the latter, Anton Hesse, is a Jew who wisely had left Germany prior to Hitler's pogroms, although his family, including his wife, perished there. As a longtime Communist, he effectively rules the group. Completely the dedicated Communist, Anton has no time for frivolity or life outside the party. He and Andrew McGrew, another airman, are the nucleus for a genuine Communist cell, with Martha and others working on various committees. A friend of Martha's, Maisie Gale, marries Andrew, since her first two husbands had died in battle; she is pregnant, though, by the son of the always-respectable local magistrate, Mr. Maynard, who comes in and out of the series and who, later, is supercilious and anxious to get his presumed grandchild. Another white colonial, the elderly Mrs. Van der Bylt (always called "Mrs. Van"), is a dedicated socialist (Labour party) and atheist, and she and Martha soon find that their causes over-lap considerably. Martha, though, has decided to marry Anton, since as an "enemy" alien, he is threatened with deportation unless his situation is made more stable. As another loveless marriage, this is also doomed to failure, and as the novel ends, the two are increasingly strained in their relationships. The formerly unified leftist organization, how-ever, has been broken up into the militants (the Commu-nists like Anton and Martha), the moderates (the Social-ists who form the Social Democratic party, which wishes to help the native Africans as much as possible under the exist-ing social structures), and the Labour party (which is allied with the white labor unions); not surprisingly, the group with which Anton and Martha are identified is the smallest and least effective, so the utter uselessness of organized ac-tivity is emphasized in their final conversations.

Landlocked begins with the war still not quite over, with Douglas remarried, with Martha's father critically ill with diabetes, and with Anton and Martha maintaining a single residence but separate identities and sexual lives, since no cohabitation can go on if a divorce is ultimately to be awarded. Maisie, now divorced from Andrew (who has been sent from the country through the influence of Mr. May-nard), is raising her daughter alone, refusing even to see the father of the child. The Cohen brothers, now discharged from the army, again start political activities, and Athen, a relocated Greek and member of the army, works actively with them. Athen, with whom Maisie is in love, is as dedi-cated as Anton, but is also aware of the necessity of the human element; later, he returns to Greece and dies in guer-rilla fighting. Various others who are also dedicated to dif-ferent leftist positions come into the novel, especially Thomas Stern, a Jewish refugee from Poland, with whom Martha has her one meaningful romantic and sexual rela-tionship. Martha's father dies, with her mother going to live with Jonathan, Martha's brother. Martha's affair with Stern continues, until he leaves for Israel; when he returns to Zambesia, he goes out into the wilderness to work and live with natives, later dying of a fever. Other valuable

members of the organization also die—such as Johnny
Lindsay, a proud old colonial utterly without racial exclusiveness—or find the postwar world far different from the
wartime—such as Jack Dobie, a former member of the par-
liament who is now labeled a Red and a "kaffir [i.e., nigger]
lover." Martha and Mrs. Van join in developing a strike of
natives, which is subsequently brutally put down, and Martha is finally divorced from Anton, who in turn discards
some of the more radical points of Communist doctrine to
become a part of established society. After attending a political meeting with her own contemporaries—a meeting
sponsored and run by fervent youths of twenty and twenty-
one, at which Martha and her friends are considered too
old to be a part—Martha prepares to leave for England and
the making of a new life.

Finally, in *The Four-Gated City*, Martha, as a rootless
new resident of London, spends her last years working as the
secretary-mistress of a noted British writer. The time covered in this novel is the approximately twenty years following Martha's emigration in 1949; but a lengthy appendix,
continuing the events in the lives of Martha and her friends,
is set in 1997, following mankind's wholesale self-destruc-
tion (both nerve gas and atomic energy are mentioned),
and it is this appendix that so frighteningly serves both to
culminate the series and to act as a portent for the civilized
world. Since so much time elapsed between the publication
of volumes four and five of the series, it is not surprising
that *The Four-Gated City* is a radical departure in several
major respects from the rest of the series; in order to provide
a valid analysis of this book, it will be discussed separately
from the rest of the series.

Throughout these volumes, as with Mrs. Lessing's other
fiction, several major themes are developed and explored.
While it cannot be said that any of the five novels deals
exclusively with any single theme, in general *Martha Quest*
is concerned with Martha's sexual awakening and self-
styled emancipation as an intelligent, well-read girl; *A
Proper Marriage* more specifically explores sex and marriage,
and, to a lesser extent, the world of politics; *A Ripple from*

the Storm is especially emphatic about politics; *Landlocked* carries forward many of the individual ideas about and discussions of black-white relationships that also inevitably occur in the earlier volumes; and *The Four-Gated City*, concerned with the mature Martha, is far less involved with race and sex and political activism; in this final volume, Martha attempts, not wholly successfully, to integrate her lifetime of experiences and reflections into the paranoid pressures of postwar England and the apocalyptic end of the world that concludes this volume. There are in addition a number of lesser themes in the first four volumes that could also warrant investigation, such as the relationships between the generations, the role played by the frequent dreams Martha and others have, and so on.

As *Martha Quest* opens, we find Martha has been reading a book on sex by Havelock Ellis, and her mother and a neighbor are complaining about the alleged laziness of native workers and the governmental regulations affecting farmers. Thus Martha's thoughts from her first appearance in the series are concerned with those areas reflecting independence and emancipation, particularly sexual, from her parents. Although the "conflict of generations" occurs frequently in Mrs. Lessing's fiction, it is in the continually strained relations between Martha and her mother that this conflict is most emphatically developed, and in which Martha's adolescent rebellion against her mother's values and restrictions can be seen as most well-founded. Although it is not until later that Martha compares herself to Ibsen's Nora in seeking "emancipation" (2:534), she from the outset is in conflict with Mrs. Quest, adding each new incident to the many others she keeps stored in her memory and by which she feels a sense of rebellion (1:77). Martha gradually accepts the reality of her mother's ideological idiosyncrasies, though she never finds herself agreeing with her. When Mrs. Quest talks nonsense about the "local Reds" (1:134), Martha counters with essentially the same meaningless retort her mother has frequently (e.g., 1:37) used against her: "Oh, don't be such a baby." Mrs. Quest habitually thinks in labels, which, because they are not the same labels

used by Martha, inevitably causes arguments; this is especially well illustrated by a letter to Martha in which the terms
"you young people," "the younger generation," "freethink-
ers," "Fabian sentimentalists," and "immoral" are repeated
in each sentence (1:239). Mrs. Quest at one time prays that
Martha will be like her conformist brother (1:69), but she
later forgets that she rebelled in much the same way against
her own mother (2:520). Dedicated as Martha's generation
is to self-knowledge (2:520), it is no surprise that she, like
so many of them, becomes "cold and logical" (2:523) in
her relationships with others. Martha had earlier been sure
that love and intelligence were necessarily related qualities
(1:195); ironically, when she consults a physician during
the start of her pregnancy, she smiles "disagreeably" at his
emphasis on her intelligence (2:531).

Especially vivid in this conflict is Mrs. Quest's own youthful rebellion, already suggested. Martha sees herself as conceived by a man in shell shock from World War I and born
to a nurse who suffered a breakdown from nursing the
wounded in that war (4:463); Mrs. Quest, awakening from
a dream, considers her own mother's objections to a career
as a nurse, i.e., to unladylike rebellion against parental authority (4:333–35), in at least one respect similar to Martha's own situation: both were pregnant when they got
married. It is therefore no surprise that Martha and other
"emancipated" women, of any generation, find themselves
so lonely and fragmented. Martha's "moral exhaustion"
makes her see herself as an "isolated person, without origin
or destination" (1:175); Douglas's mother later confesses to
the same feeling (2:377); and Martha on several occasions
(e.g., 2:387) sees herself as essentially a divided person,
akin in cause and symptoms to those experienced by Anna
Wulf in *The Golden Notebook*, discussed in a later chapter.
Martha experiences a profound loneliness during her pregnancy (2:390), and much later, in her last year or two in
Africa, she says:

There was always a point at which anything—loving
someone, a friendship, politics—one went over the edge

into . . . but she did not understand into what. Neither
the nature of the gulf nor what caused it, did she understand. But a note was struck—and that it *would* strike
could be counted on. After that . . . [4:454]

Finally, similar feelings are to be found in the dreamlife of
Martha and some other characters in this series of novels,
feelings to be discussed in greater detail later.

It is obvious, then, that Martha is self-consciously concerned with "freedom," however ill-defined this may be. As
a typist in a law office, she finds the "formal moribund language of legality" a constricting force (1:93); she discovers
that a letter from Joss "released her from her imprisonment
like the kiss of the prince in the fairy tales" (1:207); when
she and Douglas decide to marry, the decision made her
"spiritually free again" (1:234); when she first discovers
that she is pregnant, she exults in her "freedom" (2:351–
52); after Caroline's birth, she sees herself as free once again
(2:418); conventional suburban life she finds a prison
(2:510–11); and when she decides to leave her family, other
women in her circle envy her "escaping" (2:595). As a self-
styled "free spirit" (2:371, 387, 404, 405), Martha sees the
Communist party as giving women a similar freedom
(3:104), but she feels "caged and hemmed in" in her relationship with the Communist Anton Hesse (3:121). This
freedom, though, is not for her alone; she also wishes it for
others. Thus when Martha leaves her daughter, she says
that she is "setting her free" (2:600; 4:503); Martha wishes
that women could have babies if they wished to, even if they
didn't have husbands (3:114), though a friend of hers sees
herself as no longer free because of children (3:164); and
Martha subsequently feels that her freedom will not begin
until she is in England (4:506; cf. 4:453). As these references indicate, though, "freedom" as envisioned by Martha
is illusory, for each new stage of her life is anticipated as
being "freer" than the last, and each new stage is itself seen
as constricting, needing release by a further degree of "freedom."

Akin to Martha's desire for "freedom" is her fear of the

"personal," of intimate psychological involvement with another person. In reacting defensively in her typist's job to a
critical remark by her superior, she realizes her reply is too
"personal" (1:104); Donovan, the effeminate dress-designer
she dates when first in the city, could not tolerate the personal (1:150), and criticizes Martha for her immature tendency to get herself "mixed up with people" (1:153); and
her own personal problems (and those of others) are seen
to be detrimental to party work. A "personal talk" she
wishes to have with Anton becomes for him merely an item
on an agenda (3:58); and the depersonalization this implies affects her despite her supposed objectivity: "Why is
it I listen for the echoes of other people in my voice and
what I do all the time? The fact is, I'm not a person at all,
I'm nothing yet—perhaps I never will be" (3:270). She later
ponders the meaning of friendships (4:316–17); but the
conflicts inevitable in such excruciating self-analysis lead, as
suggested above, to Martha's sense of isolation and psychological division, and also to a continuous examination of
other people's probable psychological conditions. She sees
her mother, for instance, as having a life that is a "complicated system of self-denials" (2:518), and the mother herself as a "little girl deprived of something she badly wanted"
(2:522). Martha sees the group of leftists with which she
is associated as being much like the suburban wives with
whom she associated early in her first marriage (4:377),
particularly because of the manner in which others were discussed and analyzed *in absentia* (4:378–79). Such analysis,
however, is for Martha essentially self-defeating because it
substitutes the emptiness of idle conversation for the solid-
ity of commitment, of the kind of "personal commitment"
she has longed for her entire lifetime. And being so aware
of the manner in which "freedom" is postulated in her society by women like herself, it is no surprise that Martha
turns to sexual activity as the area in which her own "freedom" will be expressed.

As mentioned earlier, when we first meet Martha Quest,
she has been reading a book on sex by Havelock Ellis—"it is
hardly possible to be bored by a book on sex when one is

fifteen" (1:13). She rebuffs a lecherous older farmer when he makes advances (1:49–50), and scorns the life-denying expressions of disgust at sex, including sexual expression in art, piously made by her mother and a friend of her mother's (1:14–16). The friend's statement that "a girl must make men respect her" (1:16) and her mother's attempt to "disinfect" sex by a "humorous, teasing" tone of voice (1:72) only exasperate Martha. Mr. Quest's coming into Martha's room while she stands before a mirror bare-breasted (she is then sixteen) causes no reaction at all in either Martha or her father, but Mrs. Quest is greatly alarmed (1:26–27). Later, following a party at a well-to-do neighbor's house, Martha again has occasion to examine herself, this time before a full-length mirror.

> She had never been alone in a room with a full-length mirror before, and she stripped off her clothes and went to stand before it. It was as if she saw a vision of someone not herself; or rather, herself transfigured to the measure of a burningly insistent future. The white naked girl with high small breasts that leaned forward out of the mirror was like a girl from a legend; she put forward her hands to touch, then as they encountered the cold glass, she saw the naked arms of the girl slowly rise to fold defensively across those breasts. She did not know herself. [1:88]

Her early dating, despite her desire to rebel, is not overtly sexual in nature. One date in which Martha and several friends were crowded into a single car does serve to introduce her to erotic pleasure by means of a boy's self-conscious efforts at petting (1:80–81). At the party the group was heading toward, another boy attempts, with a "clumsy and unpracticed hand," to caress her, but is rebuffed (1:87).

Her first "serious" dating, with Donovan, previously mentioned, is wholly nonphysical and platonic. He says that "all this sex is overrated" (1:138), and Martha finds herself perfectly (and not wholly preferably) "safe" with Donovan. She is relieved that she is going to a public place with him, but, she asks herself,

for a girl whose first article of faith was that one was entitled to lose one's virginity as romantically and as soon
as possible, this was surely an odd thing to think? The
fact was, the thought of making love with Donovan was
rapidly becoming impossible, even indecent; she had
several times called him Jonathan [i.e., the name of her
brother], and never noticed the slip of the tongue. [1:139]

When Donovan designs a dress for Martha, she unselfcon-
sciously allows him to manipulate her as needed, but does
not believe him when he assures her that he will not make
love to her (1:155). Instead, after he leaves, she again in-
spects her naked body, and "soon, with frank adoration, she
fell into a rite of self-love" (1:156). She also learns how to
handle potentially erotic situations with overly-eager adolescent boys, without the attempt particularly upsetting her
(1:167), and even thinking of the sharp contrast between
the "poetic descriptions of the love act from literature, and
in scientific descriptions from manuals on sex," and the
frantic, naïve efforts to make love by the boys she dates
(1:183). She subsequently starts to date Adolph King, a
pariah in the city because of his Jewishness, and, partly out
of pity and partly because of the challenge he presents her,
she has her first experience of sexual intercourse (1:94).
This affair, though, is eminently unsatisfactory for Martha;
although she believes that she rebels against bourgeois
moral standards, even this, her first affair, suggests that the
total lack of emotional commitment in a sexual affair is
essentially self-defeating and sterile for her, as, indeed, it is
for most of Mrs. Lessing's female protagonists.

Her initial experiences with Douglas do show that Martha is in charge of the situation. Aside from one prostitute
earlier in his life, Douglas, aged thirty, had never, he says,
made love to a woman, so the prolonged description of his
first act of love with Martha (1:229–32) takes on a unique
quality. He first "in an ecstasy of humble adoration" examines her physically, only reluctantly and hesitatingly enter-
ing into intercourse. Following the act, Martha thinks:

Gallantly preserving himself for the *right* girl! How
touching. How disgusting! She tried to shut a lid on this

disconcerting spirit, and succeeded, but not before it had said derisively, in a pious voice, keeping himself clean for his wife. She turned toward him, and began caressing his head and hair in a passion of tenderness. [1:232]

Since the relationship is more physical than emotional, they decide to marry following a subsequent sexual encounter (1:234). Douglas's prudishness reminds Martha of Donovan (1:236). She also reflects about the public quality of their courtship and affair that

there was something very strange about it all, for if the point of this public orgy was sex—which surely it must be, judging from the meaning smiles, the jokes, and the way Douglas was continually taken aside by a young man, and teased until he began directing uneasy, proud, guilty looks at Martha which she tried hard not to hate him for—then sex, the thing-in-itself, had mysteriously become mislaid in the publicity. [1:237]

Douglas has indeed "mislaid" sex as Martha conceives of it, for he brings home a copy of van de Velde's *Ideal Marriage* ("It may be said that few middle-class young couples dare marry without this admirable handbook; and as Douglas had seen it in his young married friends' bookcases, he had bought it" [1:238]) and he picks from the book a particular "recipe" (i.e., position) for them to use. Only when Martha, upset, begins to cry and Douglas comforts her do they make love in a meaningful fashion without the book. Aside from these initial sexual experiences, the two do not achieve sexual harmony, because of their being "heirs" to the "English puritan tradition" (1:247). More often than not, Martha thinks of Douglas in a brotherly fashion (e.g., 1:239; 2:321), and as the marriage breaks up, so the sexual relationship is altered and gradually diminishes.

Her next sexual relationship, with Anton Hesse, is no more enduring than that with Douglas, though the marriage itself, for the various legal reasons mentioned in the plot synopsis earlier, is maintained for at least four years. Their relationship gradually grows into a sexual one, though never a satisfactory one since he suffers from premature ejaculation (3:240). Hence their carefully planned acts of sex are frequently short and violent, leaving her uninvolved. Soon, though, even this much of a tie between the two diminishes, leading both to contemplate taking lovers. The relations between Martha and Anton do improve when Anton has a mistress, only because he believes she too has a lover (4:364–65).

It is not until Thomas Stern, the displaced Jew from Poland, that Martha achieves a truly meaningful sexual relationship—and even this is abortive and relatively short-lived. Their first rendezvous in the apartment in which she and Anton live is fruitless and restrained, but later, in the loft of a small shed near his house, they regularly make love. On at least one occasion Anton has intercourse with her immediately after she has had intercourse with Thomas, simply because he knew of her infidelity (4:381), causing her to reflect that her lower inner organs did not like her being married to one man and making love with another (4:383). In the last sexual act described between the two, Thomas reverts to the same sort of desperate, violent, maniacal sex as previously had been identified with Douglas (4:434–35). He comments to Martha on one further occasion that girls like her need a "lot of serious love-making" to keep them in shape (4:467), but this affair, too, ends in as sterile and ultimately unsatisfactory a fashion as Martha's earlier liaisons.

Pregnancy and child-raising are necessarily involved in Martha's sexual experience. She dislikes the "methodical preparations" for contraception made by Adolph in her initial sexual experience (1:193), she reacts coldly to the self-conscious explanation of birth-control methods made by her physician (2:272–73), she finds even thinking about contraception, while married to Douglas, quite distasteful (2:287–88), and she later uses the lack of contraceptives as an excuse for not having sex with Douglas (2:504–5). When Martha discovers that she is pregnant with Caroline, she considers abortion but finally decides to have the child. The description of the months of pregnancy and the childbirth itself, certainly one of the most detailed and clinically precise in all fiction, culminates in Martha's again feeling "free" (2:418) and reconciled to raising the child. But Mrs. Quest plans to run the unborn child's life as completely as she had Martha's, even to the extent of choosing the name for the child (2:367) and the methods of child-raising (2:370).

The contrasts in attitudes toward sexual behavior and marriage usually, then, though not always, follow the line of demarcation between the generations, even though in practice the older women and men also have lived more freely than they advocate for their young. No doubt much of this attitude derives ultimately, as suggested earlier, from the puritan tradition in which all these characters have grown up, but, at least for Martha, there seems to be additional sources, particularly her romantic nature and her tendency to idealize whatever situation she finds herself in. For as we are told,

> Her fantasies of the night ahead centered on the intimate talk, a continuation of that existing intimacy, a complete truthfulness which would sanctify what would follow. This, however, never approached even the threshold of consciousness. At the most she imagined a kiss. But until the kiss, fantasy must sleep. She was crying out for a romantic love affair; she had been waiting for months for just this moment; not for one second had the idea entered her head. There is no such thing as a female hypocrite. [2:438]

Much of this tendency to romanticize, to exist in a fantasy situation in which such mundane realities as sex and marriage and children are subordinated to the particular dream of the moment, comes as a result of Martha's extensive reading and her tendency to conceive of particular situations in literary or other nonexperiential terms, and in dreams.

Most of Mrs. Lessing's female protagonists are widely read and frequently think in literary, especially fictional, terms. They moreover have a high degree of sensitivity to dreams, not only being able to recount their dreams—especially their nightmares—in vivid detail, but also with these dreams having either a prophetic or contrapuntal relationship to their waking lives. Martha Quest is no exception, for, as we shall see, she too demonstrates this dual capacity for image-making in literary sensitivity and dreams.

From the beginning of our introduction to Martha, we see that reading, particularly romantic reading, is an essential part of her life. Aside from the book on sex by Havelock Ellis that she was reading, she also indicates a wide familiarity with other, more literary, kinds of reading. She is said, for example, to see herself through literature; to a great extent, her dependence on reading is a result of Mrs. Quest's constant criticism and denigration of Martha as a person, for Martha, in turning away from her mother, turns toward the Quests' bookcases. We subsequently learn that Martha's mind has been formed by "poetic literature (and little else)" (1:62), and that "what she believed had been built for her by the books she read, and those books had been written by citizens of that other country," i.e., a "self-contained world which had nothing to do with what lay around her" (1:87–88). Mrs. Quest typically confuses Martha's adolescent ennui and erratic behavior with the books the girl has been reading—Shelley and Byron and Tennyson and William Morris—but thinks of them as "too respectable" to have harmful qualities for Martha (1:89–90). The "moral exhaustion" Martha feels when she sees Southern Rhodesian justice for the natives is dreadful, she believes, not because it exists but because it exists in her own day, even though the same degradation had been described by Dickens, Tolstoy, Hugo, Dostoevsky, and a dozen other writers she had read (1:176). Martha evaluates a letter from her mother in terms of the letters found in Victorian novels (1:223); she learns about what war really is through *All Quiet on the Western Front,* given her by her father (2:328–29); she evaluates an older woman's house from the pictures of England one sees in novels, especially Edwardian novels (2:332–33); she sees her town as being like a Victorian novel (2:447); she sees herself leaving Douglas as Nora would have, from Ibsen's *A Doll's House* (2:534);

she sees her sexual capacities as a novelist might have seen them (2:539–40); she compares herself to Madame Bovary (4:330–31); and she sees herself leaving her child as under-stood by writers of Victorian melodrama (4:498).

But reading for Martha serves as far more than merely a source of illustrations to apply to her life, or as escapist entertainment. She also finds that such excursions into books serve a vitally important purpose.

> Then she returned to resume that other journey of dis-covery which alternated with the discoveries of a young woman loose in town: she returned to her books. She was reading her way slowly and vaguely from book to book, on no better system than that one author might mention another, or that a name appeared in a publish-er's spring list. . . . She read as if this were a process dis-covered by herself; as if there had never been a guide to it. . . . She picked up each new book, using the author's name as a sanction, as if the book were something sep-arate and self-contained, a world in itself. And as she read she asked herself, What has this got to do with me? Mostly, she rejected; what she accepted she took instinc-tively, for it rang true with some tuning fork or guide within her; and the measure was that experience (she thought of it as one, though it was the fusion of many, varying in intensity) which was the gift of her solitary childhood on the veld: that knowledge of something painful and ecstatic, something central and fixed, but flowing. It was a sense of movement, of separate things interacting and finally becoming one, but greater—it was this which was her lodestone, even her conscience; and so, when she put down this book, that author, it was with the simplicity of perfect certainty, like the certainties of ignorance: It isn't true. And so these authors, these phi-losophers who had fed and maintained (or so she under-stood) so many earlier generations, were discarded with the ease with which she had shed religion: they wouldn't do, or not for her.

In the meantime, she continued with the process of

taking a fragment here and a sentence there, and built them into her mind, which was now the most extraordinary structure of disconnected bits of poetry, prose, fact and fancy; so that when she claimed casually that she had read Schopenhauer, or Nietzsche, what she really meant was that she had deepened her conviction of creative fatality. She had in fact not read either of them, or any other author, if reading means to take from an author what he intends to convey. [1:209–11]

When a situation presents itself for which she has no ready answers or solutions, she also finds such reading valuable therapeutically, as when her marriage to Douglas shows signs of breaking apart (2:321–22). In her own words, she slowly "tested various shells for living in, offered to her in books" (2:325), even though she eventually realizes women in novels do not seem to have quite the same problems as those she has (2:465). Gradually Martha does turn to more exclusively political and social reading, to a great extent because of the burning desire within her for a more satisfying commitment. It is in the realm of the political where Martha's reading changes most radically from her adolescent interests, though not to the degree to which it does for others in her Communist organization. Martha feels at this time as she had years earlier when the Cohens had given her books to read (3:64), i.e., as if she "had been given a gauge of trust."

Martha's subsequent reading in the realm of the political, therefore, continues with material about Japanese atrocities and African education (4:313) and the many pieces of literature sent the organization from Russia. Shortly before she leaves Africa, Martha and her compatriots read and refer respectfully to "the book," an otherwise unnamed book by Timofy Gangin, a Russian peasant who became a minor governmental official following the 1917 revolution, and who, after being imprisoned for some years, went to the United States and wrote books denouncing the Soviet Union. The book itself is immediately denounced—without being read—by some members of the organization, but Martha dutifully reads the entire book, passing it on to Anton, who reads it.

> Martha read it. If this was true, then everything she had been saying for the last seven years was a lie. But perhaps it was exaggerated?—after all, a man imprisoned unjustly was bound to be bitter and to exaggerate? that word exaggerate . . . it rang false, it belonged to a different scale of truth. Reading this book, these books, it was her first experience, though a clumsy, unsure one, of using a capacity she had not known existed. She thought: I *feel* something is true, as if I'm not even reading the words of the book, but responding to something else. She thought, vaguely, If this book were not on this subject, but about something else, well, the yardsticks I would use would say: Yes, this is true. One has an instinct one trusts, yes . . .
>
> Martha gave the book to Anton. At first he said, "I'm not going to read this trash." But he read it, dropping, as he did so, sarcastic remarks about the author's character —an unpleasant one, he said. Then he became silent. Well, nothing new about that. Martha waited, while the book lay on the table, apparently discarded. Then Anton said, "After all, they aren't saints, they were bound to make mistakes." And off he went to the Forsters, just as if he were not aware of the enormity of this remark. He did not mention the book again—and was not talking at all about Germany. [4:486]

The extensive discussion among the party members about the implications of the book (4:492–94) demonstrates not only the explosive quality of its contents, but also the divisive and fragmented quality of the group itself; some members say the book should not have been read, others say it should have as much attention as any other document, but Martha, curiously silent during the exchange, takes what appears to be a neutral stand symptomatic of her gradual disenchantment with communism. On one of her last days in Rhodesia, Martha and Mrs. Van, now alienated over the particular form of leftist political philosophy which is to prevail, debate the value and possible truthfulness of such books. For Martha, revelations about the inconsistencies of the Soviet Union are devastatingly new, whereas for Mrs. Van, a democratic Socialist, the evils of communism have never been a secret. Martha is unable to accept the fact that Mrs. Van is correct, partly, of course, because of the generation gap, but also because Martha, reacting against the Communist party, begins to go in the opposite direction, away from socialism as much as communism (4:531).

Martha's final task prior to leaving England is related to her reading in political philosophy. An old revolutionary, Johnny Lindsay, has died and has requested that his memoirs be prepared for publication (4:531–33); publication is also scheduled for the utterly chaotic memoirs of Thomas Stern, her last lover in Africa, who has died of fever while working and living with natives in an isolated place. The extensive description of the Stern memoirs (4:533–37) suggests that they were written during a state of delirium, for they contain poetry, sayings, jokes, stories, histories of African tribes, statistics, biographies and obituaries of native chieftains, obscenities, recipes, charms, tales, anecdotes, and nonsense-writing, in various colors of ink and in Polish, Yiddish, and English. The chaotic condition of these memoirs clearly makes them unfit for editing or publication, a fact that leaves Martha with a profound sense of the unreality and lunacy of the kind of commitment she had while working for leftist causes. Curiously, these personal accounts of Johnny and Thomas contrast with the naïve unreality of the highly romantic diary account Martha is described as having written when the series begins (1:16), almost as if to say to Martha that little of importance has occurred in the fourteen years separating the documents: *plus ça change, plus c'est la même chose.* In a word, though Martha's awareness of life has not altered in degree since her youth, her sense of perspective has, thus making her desire for love and happiness more akin to the "wishful thinking" of adolescence than she admits to herself.

Mrs. Van herself had gone through somewhat the same

metamorphosis in relation to both politics and reading as has Martha. As a young girl of eighteen, she had read Olive Schreiner's *The Story of a South African Farm* (1833) [3] and like her rationalist-feminist forerunner, Mrs. Van began a personal inquiry into intellectual matters (3:202–3). She thereafter read Robert Ingersoll, famed agnostic (3:203–4), and books and newspapers from both Britain and the United States. The difference between her and Martha, though, is not the reading diet itself so much as the manner with which the ideas are assimilated. For Mrs. Van always put the personal—her husband and children—first, and then retreated into periods of study, which by agreement were never interrupted by her husband. Thus she gives the appearance of being a conventionally well-to-do matron, publicly known to be a "kaffir-lover," a socialist, and a libertarian in the sense in which a democratic Socialist works through democratic procedures to effect governmental changes (3:203–6 passim).

Related to the extensive treatment of books and pamphlets is the matter of journalism, for the frequent references to newspapers of various kinds is an integral part of Martha's personal education. Even as a teenager Martha realizes that the dominant local newspaper, the *Zambesia News*, is a "disgrace" for not printing the truth about political conditions in Europe (1:220). The *News* is repeatedly described as less than accurate in its reporting of racial and political news, and is frequently caught in unacknowledged contradictions. Mrs. Van regularly collects clippings from the *News*, filed under "White Settler Imbecilities," which she sends to newspapers and magazines in other countries "as evidence of the deplorable state of affairs in Zambesia" (3:216–17). Since the *News* has no effective competition, Martha and her associates have to resort to papers from England, notably the *Observer* and the *New Statesman and Nation*; Martha's noticing Douglas reading the *New Statesman* (1:227) draws them together, just as earlier her being introduced to that newspaper made her aware of socialism (1:128–30).

As her marriage breaks up, Martha considers such questions as "What did the state of self-displaying hysteria Douglas was in have in common with the shrill, maudlin self-pity of a leader in the *Zambesia News* when it was complaining that the outside world did not understand the sacrifices the white population made in developing the blacks?" For, Martha holds, there is a connection; that is, Martha now knows for certain, if she were ever in any doubt of it, that the idealistic and romantic statements found in books and newspapers have little if any connection with what life really had to offer. Douglas is thus a part of the schoolgirl's romantic idealization of marriage, as the *News*'s maintenance of the myths of white supremacy and political expediency is the façade of an essentially immature and escapist and inhuman approach to man's relationships with his fellowman.

As suggested earlier, Martha, like Mrs. Lessing's other heroines, tends to have an extremely active dream life. These dreams not only reflect the fantasy-escape necessary to live in an essentially hostile world, but they also, particularly the nightmares, have a relationship with events in her waking hours. Other characters in this series, not surprisingly, also dream, but not usually with the detail or relevance to conscious activities and events that Martha's dreams have. Some of Martha's dreams, especially those occurring earlier in her life or in moments of relative personal tranquility, are idealistic and pleasant, as when she has a recurring dream of a "golden city . . . [a] white-piled, broad-thoroughfared, tree-lined, four-gated dignified city where white and black and brown lived as equals, and there was no hatred or violence" (1:130). But nightmares, especially those suggestive of future events in her life, are Martha's most frequent form of dreaming. She has what she calls a "private nightmare" of parents always interfering with their sons or daughters, clearly reminiscent of her own situation; she refers to this as a "great bourgeois monster, the nightmare repetition."

It was like the obsession of the neurotic who must continuously be touching a certain object or muttering a certain formula of figures in order to be safe from the malevolent powers, like the person who cannot go to bed at night without returning a dozen times to see if the door is locked and the fire out. [2:337–38]

Later, looking at her mother, Martha sees this recurring dream as "the nightmare of a class and generation: repetition."

Though Martha had read nothing of the great interpreters of the nightmare, she had been soaked in the minor literature of the last thirty years, which had dealt with very little else: a series of doomed individuals, carrying their doom *inside* them, like the seeds of a fatal disease. Nothing could alter the pattern. [2:355]

Most of Martha's dreams, though, deal with exile, especially going to a foreign land across great waters, paralleling perfectly Martha's own voluntary exile in England at the end of the fourth novel in the series. This dream first occurs when Martha is slightly ill (3:94–95), and clearly suggests Martha's profound malaise and hatred of the world in which she lives. Martha later has another nightmare.

She was on a high dry rocky place and around it washed long shoreless seas. Across this sea, which she could not reach, no matter how much she leaned and stretched out her hands, sailed people she had known. All the people she knew. [4:397]

And shortly before she and Anton are divorced, Martha has still another nightmare, "quicksand which swallowed so easily love and the living" (4:466). As the date for her departure grows more imminent, so she seems less and less sure of her future. Her next dream, described only briefly after the preceding one, is of the death of Thomas Stern, her last lover (4:468–70).

Finally, Martha has one final nightmare in which several of the same motifs as in the foregoing visions can be seen.

Outside was a steady spattering sound of falling water: The sprinkler was on, and water flung out in great arching sprays. Martha shut her eyes and listened—water, water falling, water. Somewhere was water, was rescue, was the sea. In this nightmare she was caught in, in which they all were caught, they must remember that outside, somewhere else, was light, was the sound of water breaking on rocks. Somewhere lay shores where waves ran in all day with a jostling rush like horses racing. Somewhere long fresh blue horizons absorbed ships whose decks smelled of hot salt. Martha opened her eyes. Under a deep blue sky, a flowering white bush glittered with fresh water. There were blue gulfs where white foam fell and dissolved in a hissing toss of water. Somewhere, outside this tall plateau where sudden hot rains, skies of brass, dry scents, dry wastes of grass imprisoned its creatures in a watchful tension like sleeplessness, somewhere hundreds of miles away, the ground fell, it slid to the sea. And one day (only a few months away, incredibly) Martha would quite simply, just as if this were a natural act, natural to her, that is, who had never done it, stand on a shore and watch a line of waves gather strength and run inwards, piling and gathering high before falling over into a burst of white foam. Soon. White flowers tossing against a blue sky. White foam dying in a hissing gulf of blue. White birds spreading their wings against blue, blue depths. [4:502–3]

The implications, it seems to me, are clear in these several repetitious visions of Martha's. For one thing, she seems to have a profound fear of the unknown elements in the future; and while she can visualize a probable course of action (e.g., exiling herself in England), only toward the end of her sojourn in Zambesia does this become something she can verbalize and admit to herself; it is as if the lessened inhibitions and social guardians present in her consciousness are unable to keep what is of greatest concern to her psychically from being released, from being expressed dramatically in dreams. While prophetic pertinence would be too extreme a quality to attribute to her dreams, even with the proviso that this is, after all, a fictional, not a "real," characterization, these recurring nightmares do reflect events for Martha that are yet to occur. Her dream of Thomas dying, for instance, is experienced shortly before news of his death reaches Martha. Her repeated dreaming of the same basic situation, moreover, seems to be reflective of the conflict between the ideal and the real for Martha, for she continually holds out the possibility, during her waking hours, of her romantically conceived ideal world coming to pass. As one by one these utopian wishes are seen to be unattainable, she becomes more and more expressive in her dream life of the necessity of confronting the "real," her impending self-exile, in its own terms, as a tangible and necessary event in her life. Only when she consciously admits her intent to leave for England, and only when the various attachments she has made in Rhodesia have been ended (by divorce, death, estrangement), can she again sleep without the nightmares.

Finally, Martha has one last dream, in which she conceives of herself as wandering through an increasingly dilapidated house (4:286–87), this vision is apocalyptic and suggestive for Martha, for her own house, the one in which the Quests lived, becomes dilapidated and vermin-infested when Mr. Quest dies and Mrs. Quest moves north to live with Martha's brother, Jonathan. Thus, the ability to conceive of images of her own life in dreams becomes in a way the same as in her extensive reading—both a means of escaping from the realities of the present and a method of looking to the future.

Now, as the foregoing comments indicate, Martha first considered political and social radicalism through her reading. Her tendency to react against the authority of her elders, repeatedly seen in the chapters devoted to her teenage years, is likely also an influence, for when Donovan, her effeminate first boyfriend, warns her about being mixed up with the local Reds, a group he implies is made up mostly of Jews, Martha reacts, both in dating Adolph, a Jew, and in becoming more active herself in leftist activities. The disapproval of others, even her own contemporaries, toward radical political movements is such that Martha feels more strongly interested in such movements (see, e.g., 2:279–80, 345), just as she stubbornly reacts when she is accused of being a pacifist (2:317). Armed with facts from the *New Statesman*, Martha engages in her first political argument while working in an office as a secretary; she firmly declares that it is Franco, not the republicans, who are the true rebels in Spain (1:211–12), but discovers that such arguments are impossible to win. Solly Cohen's refusal to join the Communist party (he is a Trotskyist) she also finds causes a reaction in her, for immediately following the discussion (2:303), she is invited by him to attend a meeting that evening; since Solly is jesting, Martha is upset, but again is more receptive to such a meeting when it does occur. Her reasons for becoming identified with leftist organizations, then, spring both from her romantic, idealistic temperament which wishes to see injustices rectified, and from the indifferent and antagonistic manner others in her circle of acquaintances demonstrate toward leftist activities. Mr. Quest tells Douglas that Martha was a Socialist, "which was not important," she says, "since it was only a disease natural to her age" (1:242); he adds that she is an atheist as well, and Mrs. Quest later says that Martha has no patriotism (2:355). It is, therefore, not wholly surprising that Martha chooses to affiliate with a Communist organization.

Actually joining the group, however, requires more than mere desire, as Martha soon discovers. Although welcome to attend and work, Martha is the wife of a civil servant; thus when the opportunity to join is mentioned, she is told that there are difficulties because of her sports club crowd, and that because of the "change" in the "atmosphere" (i.e., Russia being allied in the war effort with the commonwealth), even wives of civil servants should be aware of the current situation (2:536). After Martha examines some old newspapers to discover for herself the changes in the political climate, she sees that the group, however it was constituted at the time, was finally "doing something"—but what, she asks? (2:538). She then asks William, an airman also in the group, "Look. You don't have to—flannel, like this. If there's a Communist group, I want to join it" (2:547). When he tells her there is no Communist party group, she is disappointed, but he explains that he never joined because he had reservations about past policies of the party, evidently the Stalin-Hitler pact. Several front organizations are begun, with another airman wishing to start a genuine Communist group, when Anton, a Communist since 1933, and Andrew, one since 1930, assume charge.

Anton finally does get the nucleus of would-be party members together, addressing them and discussing the world's problems from a Marxist viewpoint, for most of them the first such address they have heard (2:571); after a majority vote supports the establishment of a party group, it is made official (2:575). Martha's subsequent feelings of "exasperated boredom," she believes, would not be approved by Anton, for mere membership in the party did not make one a real Communist (2:585). From the outset, though, splinter Marxist sympathy, especially Trotskyist, must be faced. Solly Cohen and several other local Communists are identified as Trotskyists (2:551, 3:82), and Jasmine (Solly's cousin) soon denounces Solly for such an ideology (2:569). Solly had himself left the Stalinist camp because of the Stalin-Hitler pact (2:369), but none of the ordinary party members know the difference between a Stalinist and a Trotskyist, and indeed know only partial truths about Trotsky himself (3:44–45). The Trotskyists themselves have little in common and are actually hostile to each other (3:45). The air force members denounce alleged deviationism such as Trotskyism in a memorandum to the party chapter (3:161), and Solly later establishes relations with a native leader intended to rival the native leader selected by the more "conventional" leftists (4:442). Anton refuses to attend the same meeting as Solly, because of his being a "Trotskyist traitor" (4:487). Following the dissolution of a group of respectable local religious and political leaders which had been established to support the "Sympathizers of Russia" committee, the group discusses party policy and a further committee. Since both factions are able to raise significant amounts of money for Russian aid, the antagonism is not as great as the leaders of each would expect or desire, being limited to snide remarks made socially. And since both factions ultimately dissolve, with their members in either case becoming a part of the "respectable" elements of society, the antagonism seems less than clearcut or precise.

The party structure and outreach do not, however, operate on purely doctrinal grounds, even though Anton Hesse, its nominal leader, is the epitome of the bureaucratic leader more concerned with procedure than with results. The exact motives for becoming a Communist in this particular group range from wanting to be different (3:124), to feeling a sense of camaraderie with those in other nations (3:37), to a quasi-religious mystique (2:545–46), to a vague concern for the "truth" (3:83), to the supposed unanimity of conclusions two Communists on opposite sides of the world would inevitably achieve (3:187), to the opportunity to put social ethics into organized action (3:90–91), to the necessity for mutual assistance, support, and criticism (3:109, 129–35), to the logicality and rightness of communism (3:60). Membership in the party itself implies that the individual members will be concerned with good health (3:59), with regarding membership as a matter of life and death (3:87), with bravery (4:532), with always putting the party first (3:242), with freedom (3:163), with "respectability and goodness" (3:40), and with reliability, punctuality, and eagerness to work hard (3:46–47). And Anton gives a lengthy portrait, in panegyric terms, of the Communist mystique as he sees it (3:40). In short, to be a Communist as far as the impassioned rhetoric of such leaders as Anton is concerned is to encompass within one personality all the virtues and strengths imaginable to man. Small wonder that no single person, including Anton himself, is able to meet these difficult criteria!

Anton is himself so dedicated a Communist that his fervent behavior becomes a caricature of fanaticism, and his jargon-laden speaking the *reductio ad absurdum* of the bureaucrat. Anton's usual suggestion for the group is for them to have a series of lectures, preferably by himself, on party doctrine or history, an idea that does not win much enthusiasm. Martha says to Jasmine at one time, "we talk and talk and analyze and make formulations, but what are we doing? What are we changing?" (3:98). One party member tells Anton that he is the "image of a bureaucrat," which Anton concedes (3:133–34). So impractical are some of the bureaucratic suggestions made by Anton and others like him that one of the group's members, Piet, later to leave it for a respectable, indeed capitalist, occupation, says aloud and in a jocular manner:

> "Well, we can take over the Government any day now. All we need is to explain to our white fellow citizens that we're the men for the job. After all, we don't seem to have any Africans with us, do we?" Anton frowned, but said nothing. For some time Piet had been making remarks of this nature; he had become the privileged clown of the group, who could say things no one else could. [3:186–87]

Such a half-humorous reaction to matters considered deadly serious by the party faithful is quite the same as described in *The Golden Notebook* when a particular member speaks the forbidden truths all the others in the group recognize but are hesitant to express, and who gets away with making such statements because they are expressed in a joking manner.

Shortly before Martha leaves Southern Rhodesia for England, she, Jasmine, and Marjorie, three of the remaining devoted leftists in the original group, attend a meeting of younger, impassioned men and women who desire the same things that Martha's group had several years previously. She observes the same types of people attending this meeting as had attended those she recalls from the war years, particularly the moderator:

> So if history was repeating itself—and why not? If the dramatis personae were the same, presumably the plot was also—this group would not be in existence, these people would not sit all night on uncomfortable benches

talking about nation-wide networks which would trans-
form the country, if it had not been for the impassioned
orator? [4:539]

She sees the transfigured expressions of those listening in-
tently to the moderator, thinking that they came as "representatives of common sense," and having a "restraining influence" on their society, just as before. But she realizes that
the speaker will have his own way in planning and in emphasizing the "vision" they are to keep in mind at all times.
As he continues with "an analysis of the situation," Martha
realizes that the speaker and Anton are alike (4:542), except that the topic of conversation for the younger group,
reflecting the changed times, was the effect likely to be had
by Communist China on the world scene. The young people respectfully request Jasmine, as a member of the de-
funct Communist party in South Africa, to sum up the discourse, which she does at some length (4:543). When
Jasmine finishes, the three older girls, recognizing the feeling of a "closed meeting" scheduled next, rise and leave.
Marjorie, continually hopeful, says: "Oh, I'm so pleased
they are starting. It doesn't make one feel so bad about our
failing. And if only they'll learn some lessons from our mistakes" (4:554). But Martha, recognizing what she cannot
express, that is, the passing of the old way and the necessity
of changing with it, vanishes from sight at the corner, leaving Southern Rhodesia and, presumably, the Communist
cause, for good.

Thus Martha Quest has come full circle from her adolescent interest in reacting against authority; first interested in
radical social and political thought through books lent her
by friends who were themselves representatives of a persecuted people, Martha has moved to full and active involvement in Communist affairs and subsequently to voluntary exile from both the country in which leftist activities
are proscribed and presumably from the leftist cause itself.
Her reasons, though, seem not to be mere cowardice or fear
of persecution, the reasons given by others, particularly civil
servants and members of the establishment, but rather a

profound sense that the years as a Communist have really accomplished very little. The nostalgic feeling of helplessness she experiences when attending the meeting of the younger would-be Communists suggests that these persons, too, will have to discover for themselves the exact meaning of their political experiences. For Martha, though, the commitment to communism, although never formally and abruptly concluded, does diminish and is gradually dissipated in other activities. For the one cause she has been continually concerned in, the cry for racial justice and equity, is no closer to satisfactory resolution at the end of the fourth novel in this series than it had been at the beginning of the first, though Martha does find in *The Four-Gated City* that the basic problem in racial relationships is no different in England than it has been in Africa. Nonetheless, her continuing interest in the subject of race, surpassing even her political interests in degree of dedication, warrants some remarks.

When Martha is twenty-one years of age, she realizes that she has never "sat in a room with a dark-skinned person as an equal," even though her entire life had been spent in a colony with nine-tenths of the population considered "dark-skinned" (2:449). Although Martha had grown up hearing the conventional white suspicions about the charges against the natives, she repeatedly reacts against such statements, in particular against her mother's continually suspicious treatment of native servants; Mrs. Quest criticizes, for instance, Martha's own servants (during her marriage to Douglas) for laziness and the perpetually suspected erotic interest the servants are presumed to show to white females; when words cannot come to express her feelings, she explodes, "Filthy creatures!" (2:518, see also 2:516–17, 522). Hence Martha's early desire to destroy such words as "black," "white," "nation," and "race" (1:57), although naïvely idealistic, do suggest the very real desire in her to achieve harmony and justice for all mankind, at least one of her reasons for identifying with Communists and Socialists, as the foregoing remarks indicate.

At first, Martha is herself as wrapped up in abstract expressions of racial peace as her parents are with racial hatred. At a party with her teenage friends, she tries to tell her host, the man who had visited her parents earlier, that "she believed in equal rights for all people, regardless of race," only to be cut off by a boy who wants her to dance (1:86). Mr. Player, a noted and respected white man, later impresses Martha with his expression of views which he knew would be challenged by 90 percent of his white audience (2:313). The fact of unequal treatment especially concerns Martha, whether it be inequitable earning power, restricted benches in a public park, the use of passes, or punishment. Martha had frequently seen the use of required passes, but suddenly she is hit with the angry realization that the use of passes is the kind of oppression found in a police state (1:176). Mr. Maynard, the magistrate, recounts a case he had heard on a particular morning in which a native had stolen some clothes from his employer and for which the punishment was either prison or a beating; after a listener says "Nonsense, they should all be whipped!", Mr. Player says that "the whole legal system as affecting the Africans was ridiculously out of date and should be radically overhauled" (2:310; cf. 3:116–17). Maynard says in reply that the natives did not mind prison, so whipping served more effectively as punishment; after all, he says, the natives were nothing but children (2:310–11). Martha is struck by the fact that two familiar words—"nigger" and "kaffir"— have not been used in the discussion, which continues with well-meaning statements by young persons from England criticized in turn by the older listeners as ill-informed and clearly affected by residence in England. Mr. Player, putting the conversation more in business than social terms, says that the whites were hurting themselves economically, for if the natives were not to revolt, they must have decent food and housing (2:311–12).

Invariably introduced in white comments about the blacks is the sexual fear suggested above. Mrs. Quest warns Martha about potential attacks from natives (though she cannot bring herself to say the word "rape"), with Martha quickly retorting that a white man who had raped a black girl the previous weekend received only a five pound fine (1:49). Mr. Maynard says in a group of whites that in England the natives "are treated as equals . . . even by the women," not having to say more than this to make his point (2:315). When Mrs. Quest suggests that Martha get a boy to help her shop, Martha replies with the same comment her mother had frequently used toward her: "I thought you said it was dangerous to have a boy in a place where there was a small girl because he was bound to rape her?" (2:436). And Mrs. Carson, Martha's landlady, expresses her psychotic, obsessive fear of black men looking through the windows at white women (3:96, 100), combined with what is evidently a simultaneous desire to be violated (3:30–31). Martha catches herself thinking of "girl" as meaning "white girl" when she and another party member walk along a street in the "Coloured" section (3:74–75). Childbirth for the native women, Martha's white suburban housewife friends tell her, is different than for the whites: "They're not civilized, having babies is easy for them, everyone knows that. . . . everyone knows they are nothing but animals, and it doesn't hurt them to have babies" (2:279–80).

The generally superior attitude of the whites is expressed in numerous ways in Martha's experience, with a white journalist saying he is convinced that the "mass of the blacks" only want to be left alone (3:235). By contrast, Johnny Lindsay, an old white settler, has completely abolished the "Colour Bar" in his own house (4:387). Since the Africans, according to Mrs. Van, lack self-confidence, they must be given the opportunities "to be as cruel and stupid as we are," and so she intends to teach them African history. But, she discovers, the Africans had no official history, nor anything from any governmental or educational source that could serve as one, so Johnny Lindsay, who had been in the country as an active observer of the racial scene since before the turn of the century, provides an oral history transcribed by Martha (4:389–95).

Given this highly emotional, irrational attitude of the whites toward the natives, and especially toward a potential native uprising, then, one can easily see the fears of the

whites when an actual organized strike occurs. The initial
radio announcement of the threat of such a strike, despite
the frequency with which it has been a topic of conversation, seems almost fantasy (4:506). In all the colony's
seventy years of "history"—i.e., white occupation (4:509) —
there had been nothing like this well-organized though
wholly illegal strike. Panic-stricken whites who unreason-
ably assume it is a revolution talk and behave in completely
uncivilized ways (4:507, 511, 513), suggesting as a solution
the imprisonment or deportation of the strike leaders instead of mere talk (4:516). White landowners in out-of-the-
way parts of the colony report that no racial disturbances
would have occurred in the cities if the natives hadn't been
taught to read (4:518). In the cities such as Zambesia, all
natives who have not run away are herded into enclosures;
but no one is allowed out of the enclosures, and almost no
food is brought into them (4:527, 529). The strike finally
collapses a few days later, not because of lack of food so
much as the absurdity of a situation in which blacks were
imprisoned because of the authorities' fears of white retalia-
tion (4:529).

In this strike as in other social unrest, the local Communist group plays an active part. Communism itself had
been considered free of race prejudice, including anti-
Semitism (3:31), leading a number of prominent local
whites to believe that the local group was "putting ideas"
into the natives' minds (3:56, 74, 77). The reactions of the
members of the local group range from the expected denun-
ciation of white supremacy (3:126, 195; 4:441), to a member's honest and abrupt confession of lingering prejudice
(3:80, 227), to the extremist comment of an R. A. F. member of the group who feels Anton's advice to avoid affairs
with the "Coloureds" in the town is itself a racist attitude
(3:109). The party can work behind the scenes in such an
endeavor as the strike, but cannot publicly take a part in
the establishment of native organizations, even though such
indigenous organizations do on occasion arise (e.g., 3:190).

Several specific African leaders are mentioned in the
series who are responsible for such activities as these native

organizations. Mentioned earlier was Mr. Matushi, whose astute handling of potentially tense racial situations is suggested by both his discussion with Mr. Maynard, also mentioned earlier, and his intelligent comment following a lecture on world economic conditions. Matushi says that many of his people would be interested in knowing that whites in England have problems in housing and diet, and that the natives, if they had such information, might not "be so hurt by the newspapers when they said all black men were centuries in evolution behind the white men" (3:452). Matushi's indispensability for the native cause is suggested by his active and necessary involvement in numerous different organizations (3:190) and his linguistic virtuosity (3:243). When Johnny Lindsay gives an oral history of the colony, Matushi is the one who encourages him to continue, for "It is important for us all that we should know these things, even though it [i.e., the Boer War] was a battle between white men" (4:394). Another African leader, Mr. Zientli, is more militant and causes fears to arise in many white people (4:350, 357). Zientli is involved with Solly Cohen's Trotskyist group (4:442), and is considered too extreme to effect any lasting improvements in the racial situation.

Caught between the whites and the blacks, and in many ways the most unfortunate group of all, are the "Coloureds," the mulattoes. Their rejection by both color extremes inevitably makes them unstable (2:301), the alleged source of most of the petty criminals (2:428), accused of rampant venereal disease (2:428), and forced to live in a particularly congested area unchanged since the previous century (2:584). Most "Coloured" children die in their first year, Martha observes, and in general the half-caste group lives as nine-tenths of the rest of the world lives, that is, under substandard conditions (2:584–85, 589). Some of the Communists plan a concert to raise money for the "Coloureds" (2:560), a plan never carried out. Despite the congested conditions in the "Coloured" quarter, it is seriously suggested by Mr. Maynard that even more half-caste children be born so that the authorities will be forced to provide better living conditions for them (2:428).

One major group of people is generally lumped with those with Negro blood in the thinking of many white Rhodesians, a group with which Martha has frequent contact: Jews. As indicated, many of Martha's closest friends and most of her lovers are Jewish: Joss, Solly, and Jasmine Cohen, Adolph King, Anton Hesse, and Thomas Stern. While still in her midteens, Martha reacts against this particular form of prejudice (1:23), especially when her father accepts unquestioningly accusations against the Jews (1:36). As noted earlier, Solly gives Martha a book on the Jewish question which she reads (1:47), and she and Joss discuss anti-Semitism, finding themselves in agreement (1:52–53). She stops seeing Donovan after he accuses all the local leftists of being Jewish (1:134, 218). Martha's circle of friends includes Andrew and his wife, Stella, a Jewess (1:170–72), who is herself among those warning Martha of Adolph King, a Jewish band member (1:181) whom Martha deliberately chooses to date. Thomas later recounts a sadistic sergeant's anti-Semitic statements (4:411) and his own fight with the sergeant, who has only two words in his vocabulary: kike and Jew (4:413). Thomas calls himself a wandering Jew because of his peripatetic travels around the world trying to find a home (4:429), and also presumably because of the suffering he deliberately seeks (4:512, 536). In short, the racial situation in the country is such that even those who are Jewish are self-conscious and aware of the degrees of prejudice that could be directed toward them as easily as toward the blacks. The traditional sense of suffering sometimes identified with Judaism is seen not only in the sense in which most of those identified as Jews become even more distinguished from their countrymen by becoming Communists, but also by Martha's vicarious identification with Jews by her frequent choice of Jews as lovers.

No matter how high-minded might be Martha's desires to work and live equitably with those of other races, persecuted as they are by the dominant white majority, she finds out that Southern Rhodesia is neither willing nor ready for a social revolution. Moreover, the abortive efforts made by the Communist party and the native leaders themselves suggest to her that the situation will gradually worsen before any amelioration occurs. For her, then, this commitment, as with those to radical political involvement and an intelligent well-read status as an "emancipated" person, cannot continue in the same manner as it had previously. Thus her emigration to England, presumably both an escape to a better country and to a more meaningful and lasting personal (romantic and sexual) commitment, carries with it both the recollection of the commitments made in Africa and the hope that she can reconcile her idealistic hopes and the practical necessities of living in a new land.

Many of the points made regarding the life of Martha Quest in the foregoing pages of this chapter find even further support in the final volume in the series, *The Four-Gated City*, treated separately below. For Martha Quest, despite her occasionally unpleasant and tiresome qualities—her occasional rebelling for the sake of rebellion, her enduringly romantic outlook on life in which a better situation is always seen just ahead, her rare satisfaction with what she has in life, her self-conscious intellectualization of the personal, and so on—continues the quest implicit in her surname, the quest for a better commitment, for a wholly satisfying sexual experience, for an outlet for her idealistic tendencies. Martha's successive rejection of respectable suburban marriage, of political activism, of the racial cause, thus indicates her own uncertainty and dissatisfaction with the life available to her. Moreover, as an intelligent observer of the African situation, she can easily see the impossibility of lasting, viable political progress or racial justice in a nation where all the presumed enlightenment during the war years, the direct product of Communist activity, is dissipated as if it had never occurred. Her leaving is therefore not cowardice but a resignation to the inevitable and a step toward realizing her potential in a different, less alien, environment. And although it has been mentioned on occasion that Martha appears much like Emma Bovary—her extensive romantic reading, her casual affairs, her rebellion against bourgeois standards and values—there is none of Emma's concern with self in Martha, who normally finds fruitful living in the political and social realms. Had it not been for this effort to reach out to others in her life, Martha no doubt could have developed the same kind of ingrown soul that Emma had, and consequently chosen death to disappointment.

At least a portion of this series does derive from another source, however, the same probable source singled out for *The Grass Is Singing*: D. H. Lawrence. In the last months of her pregnancy, Martha and another girl, Alice, also in the final stages of pregnancy, go out into the country during a rainstorm and commune with nature, in a scene that ideally should be quoted at length (2:394–96). The sense of "freedom" this experience gives the two women is more than a little like the experience shared by Ursula and Gudrun in Lawrence's *Women in Love*,[4] when the two sisters swim freely in the nude, then, like nymphs, dry themselves and dress.[5] Following their swim, the sisters sing and act playful together, after which Gudrun dances erotically before some cattle. In both cases the two women swim in the nude, followed by erotic movements before animals clearly suggesting fertility; in the case of Martha and Alice, their grotesquely misshapen pregnant bodies are seen in relation to the spawn of a frog, as full of potential life as the two women themselves. Martha, moreover, sees a green snake slithering along through the grass as part of this fruitful scene, certainly reminiscent of (though not directly reflective of) Lawrence's poem, "Snake." The poem also concerns a snake in the presence of water, reminding the narrator in the poem of the dignity and divinity of the snake, and also of the relationship it has to the forbidden natural wisdom available only in small degree to man.

The suggestion has also been made, as one final example of possible borrowing from Lawrence, that the shed near Thomas Stern's house in which he and Martha make love is similar to the situation in *Lady Chatterley's Lover*, in which such lovemaking also occurs.[6] The parallel does exist between the two books, it is true, with the major similarity being the principal characters: Stern is the rugged peasant who enables Martha, involved in a loveless and sexless marriage, to find sexual fulfillment. One can only point out this parallel, however, not assume direct influence or borrowing, unlike the probable situation with the *Women in Love* example.

In some respects, Mrs. Lessing's series seems like the very kind of novel that in the chapter on *The Golden Notebook* will be described as old-fashioned. In that work, Mrs. Lessing describes her protagonist's writing a novel as a means of achieving psychic health, and with the novel beginning conventionally: "The two women were alone in the London flat." In the *Children of Violence* series, we have comparable initial sentences: "Two elderly women sat knitting on that part of the verandah which was screened from the sun by a golden shower creeper" (*Martha Quest*); "It was half past four in the afternoon. Two young women were loitering down the pavement in the shade of the sunblinds that screened the shopwindows" (*A Proper Marriage*); "From the dusty windows of a small room over Black Ally's Cafe it could be seen that McGrath's ballroom was filling fast" (*A Ripple from the Storm*); "The afternoon sun was hot on Martha's back, but not steadily so; she had become conscious of a pattern varying in impact some minutes ago" (*Landlocked*); and "In front of Martha was grimed glass, its lower part covered with grimed muslin. The open door showed an oblong of browny-grey air swimming with globules of wet" (*The Four-Gated City*). In each case we have a traditional introduction not only emphasizing the observations of a woman or, more frequently, two women, but also the obvious emphasis on the perceptivity and perspectives of the women. Though these are traditional, even commonplace Victorian beginnings for a novel, Mrs. Lessing proceeds from such inauspicious statements to fashion a lasting examination of the continuing life of a far from conventional woman.[7]

The temptation to which many reviewers of the volumes in the *Children of Violence* series succumbed in identifying Martha Quest with Mrs. Lessing herself is an easy and superficially justifiable, though erroneous, conclusion. Martha's intellectual development and self-exile from her homeland parallels in many ways the circumstances in which Mrs. Lessing herself has been a part. But Martha's changing thinking and activities suggest, I believe, something of greater significance for the series as an extended work of fiction than merely an author's creation of a *persona* that is intentionally autobiographical. Martha, like Anna Wulf in *The Golden Notebook*, is consciously set up as the prototype of the sensitive modern woman who finds the easy answers about sex, politics, and so forth, given her by a masculine society less and less satisfying. The only recourse for such a woman, then, is to rebel, first in overt ways against the mores and established principles of thinking and behaving, and later is more dramatic, immutable ways, such as deliberate social action designed to better the conditions of those abused by established society, and, finally, by leaving the country for a presumed better world elsewhere. This self-styled emancipation is, however, somewhat more complicated a reaction than the merely rebellious seeking after freedom one finds in, say, Mary McCarthy, with whom Mrs. Lessing is sometimes compared. Miss McCarthy, for instance, sometimes presents women who adventurously try to act "free" sexually by having casual affairs or by getting divorced because it is a "fashionable" thing to do (e.g., the story " 'Cruel and Barbarous Treatment' "); but Mrs. Lessing's heroine, whatever her name or peculiar circumstances, continually attempts to arrive at an ideal sexual relationship and thus is less promiscuous in intent than a number of Miss McCarthy's heroines.

Idealism is similarly seen in Mrs. Lessing's characters' involvement politically. Perhaps best exemplified in a minor novel briefly discussed later, *Retreat to Innocence*, this trait leads this prototypal heroine to identify herself with radical social and political movements as a means of bringing about a corrective to the many injustices in the civilized world. True, disillusionment inevitably sets in, but little of the indifferent cynicism again to be found in Miss McCarthy is noticed in Mrs. Lessing's characters. In other words, while the realization that this is not a perfectible world has to be accepted by these heroines, the reaction is not one in which all values and goals are discarded as ineffective. Martha Quest leaves Rhodesia not because she has changed in goals or given up in the drive to make these goals visible, but rather because she realistically accepts the inevitability and effective control of the white colonial way of life, and so relocates in an attempt to follow her ideals in a more compatible atmosphere. In this respect Mrs. Lessing's prototypal heroine seems to me to be representative of many such characters in modern fiction: combining the idealistic, romantic fervor of a heroine from the Victorian era with the blasé, sophisticated, and self-consciously emancipated qualities of a modern woman, this heroine, whatever she is named, pushes inexorably on to the individual decision she alone must make, a decision not to fight blindly against overwhelming odds nor to give up when opposing forces first confront her, but rather to attempt in a wholly dedicated manner to bring about in practice her ideals and then to adjust her tactics when the situation in which she finds herself is altered.

To summarize, then, one can see how Martha has developed in the first four volumes in this series from a self-confident though inexperienced teenage girl to a self-assured and relatively "free" woman. Martha discovers in the fourteen or so years of her life described in the series thus far that she cannot live without the "personal element," and that to a great extent this derives from her contact with those she meets who seem representative of the natural or spontaneous in life. And Martha, when pregnant and ill with labor pains, contrasts the coldly clinical efficiency of the nurses (representatives of objective science and unfeeling impersonality) in the lying-in hospital, who refuse to do anything to help her pain, with an old African scrub woman who smiles at Martha, lays her hand on Martha's distended abdomen, and tells her to "let the baby come" as if she were crooning to one of her own culture. Martha's visible relaxation and submission to her condition enables her to deliver her child without complications (2:406). That is, the native woman's oneness with the natural becomes for Martha the means by which life can continue.

In much the same way, the ineffectual efforts at express-
ing the continuation of life in other respects (such as the
frantic, selfish, clinical sexual gropings of some of her lovers)
found in Martha's experience lead her to discard such areas
of her life as the respectable suburban housewife's status
and instead to choose a life in which the personal element
is paramount. One particular incident in *Landlocked* suggests this quite well: Martha deliberately chooses to identify
and remain friends with Maisie, despite the sloppy, appalling
conditions in which Maisie lives, rather than to cooperate
in the Maynards' plan to get Maisie's child for themselves
(their son is the father of the child). The natural, con-
tented relationship between Maisie, her mother, and her
child sharply contrasts with the distant and uninviting scene
Martha envisions in the Maynards' life, or, for that matter,
in her own mother's life as well. When the political and
racial situation changes to the point where personal relationships with any degree of equality are no longer possible
between blacks and whites, or for that matter between people of various political viewpoints, she finds it impossible
to remain any longer in Rhodesia. The Communist party,
despite its high-sounding preaching and hard work, has in
reality accomplished nothing that will last; the racial situation has deteriorated from what it had been during the war
years; those likely at one time to have effected social and
political change are either dead, gone, politically defeated,
or worn out and nearing the end of their active lives (e.g.,
Mrs. Van). It thus seems to Martha that one must either
conform to the mindless joviality of the sports club crowd
or to the masochistic ineffectuality of the leftists. Since
Martha has had the courage and the perspective to see
both her past and likely future in the colony, she realizes
that the alternatives open to her are either to stay in the
colony (and stagnate) or leave for England (and hopefully
once again to achieve personal meaning in life).

Despite the clarity of insight into Martha's situation, the
depth with which we are able to see her sexual, intellectual,
political, and social lives, and the precision with which the
various stages of a woman's life are lived from adolescence

to maturity, the first four parts of the *Children of Violence* series still present a woman who is only partially "free," who is still quite fragmented in her ability to reconcile opposing elements in her own life, and who has not yet achieved either true independence or true commitment. Such commitment and freedom do occur for Martha when she emigrates to England; indeed, so unusual and crafted is Mrs. Lessing's account of Martha's maturity and ultimate aging and death in *The Four-Gated City* that this novel warrants separate treatment.

Little could the reader of the first four volumes of the *Children of Violence* series have envisioned the final volume when it appeared in 1969, even though, as already mentioned, it was obvious that it would deal with Martha Quest's mature years away from the Africa of her childhood and early adulthood. Rather than deal merely with the same issues as in the earlier novels, however, Mrs. Lessing presents in *The Four-Gated City* a searing picture of postwar London, the chaos and confusion of the 1950s and 1960s, and finally a devastatingly apocalyptic portrait of the end of both the twentieth century and civilization itself, as a means of portraying the dissolution of the entire mad mentality of our world. Though many readers of the earlier volumes in the series felt that she had lost interest in the adult Martha Quest, it now seems evident that Mrs. Lessing had laid the foundations for the culminating volumes as early as the publication of the first. The title itself, for instance, although it seems to apply variously to London or a vision from the Revelation of John, actually is first mentioned in the initial volume of the series in a recurring dream of Martha's about a "golden city whose locality was vague . . . the white-piled, broad-thoroughfared, tree-lined, four-gated, dignified city where black and white and brown lived as equals, and there was no hatred or violence" (1:130). As we shall see, however, such a utopian vision is ironically inverted in the final pages of this novel, in an epilogue certain to be referred to frequently in future discussions of dystopian fiction. Mrs. Lessing said in an interview [8] following this novel's publication that the book is not fantasy, but instead is what is likely to happen to a race of mankind that is corrupted, violent, perverted, and brutal. As such, it constitutes a most appropriate culmination to the series and gives a much more fitting (though equally ironic) sense of the meaning of the title *Children of Violence* itself than to use it merely to refer to the alienated youth between the world wars in colonial Africa.

After arriving in London in 1949, Martha Quest is at first rootless and insecure. In time she becomes secretary to a writer named Mark Coldridge, general overseer to his household, and, eventually, his mistress as well. The Coldridges, a genteel Bloomsbury family, so occupy Martha's time that she becomes considerably more subdued than one would have anticipated in expressions of her own convictions. To be sure, she still is concerned with the world of ideas, but she is far more of a passive observer than an active manipulator of her environment. For some twenty years she is thus occupied, until certain catastrophe seems imminent upon England. Coldridge himself then leaves—ironically, for Africa, where he intends to establish a sanctuary for those who survive the Armageddon he prophecies—and Martha and Mark's insane wife Lynda find cooperation in mutual survival in England paramount in their lives. Much of Martha's subsequent awareness of the meaning of existence grows out of her relationship with Lynda, who will be discussed further in this chapter, but for the moment it is sufficient to note the increasingly difficult task involved in distinguishing the sane from the insane in the world Mrs. Lessing presents. The 1970s, we are told, are the decade in which the British Isles are destroyed by a cataclysmic event never quite specified. Then, in the final pages, set in the 1990s, we learn that Martha has died in a holocaust caused by an accidental touching-off of atomic weaponry or releasing of nerve gas, as if to suggest —again, with heavy irony—that what man sometimes tries to avoid doing deliberately he accomplishes through accident or carelessness.

Martha is as preoccupied as previously with a self-conscious awareness of the world around her, particularly with the inexorable passing of time; in the portions of the book concerned with the 1950s and 1960s, numerous specific incidents (such as the Korean conflict, the McCarthy vendetta, the death of Stalin, the Hungarian revolt, a London peace march, and the advancing ages of her parents and daughter) serve to set the book specifically in time. The contrast between colonial Africa and London is also firmly implanted in Martha's mind, with her initial response after arriving in England one of apologist about the real Africa as a means of countering the misconceptions held by native Britons; at one point, when Mrs. Quest is visiting Martha in London, Martha notes the reaction of both her mother and native Londoners to the presence of two black Kenyans (5:262–63). She also discovers that attitudes formerly shared by only a small number of people regarding African racial matters have in fact spread to the level of "well-informed opinion" (5:346–47), and that her old friend Joss Cohen, after years of unwilling exile from Africa, was an embarrassment to the new native governments when he returned to that continent (5:457–58). But racial matters, although important enough to be developed in more detail below, do not concern Martha as much as political and sexual matters do, nor even, for that matter, as much as Martha's increasing interest in psychic experience, particularly extrasensory perception.

The transition from one nation and social system to another, despite a similarity in language spoken, becomes for Martha a considerably more involved operation as a result of her political convictions. Early after her arrival in London, she encounters a Labour party member, Mark's sister Phoebe, who simultaneously desires the dissolution of classes in society and suspects Communists, who presumably share this goal, to be dangerous fanatics. After a conversation with Phoebe, Martha decided that "if she were going to have to be political, Communism was nearer her mark than 'Labour' in its various degrees" (5:80); when Phoebe becomes too aggressive in soliciting Martha's services, Martha withdraws from her desire for involvement in the Labour party. She then discovers that one could deter-

mine someone else's political bias from that person's attitude toward television (5:139–40). As had happened in
Rhodesia, the various leftists were disunified and split into
competing factions that tended both to weaken them as an
effective force and to belie their flaunted concern for the
common man; still, the Labour party, Martha is told, will
again come to power (5:454–59 passim). But it is communism that continues at first to have the greatest appeal
for Martha. Early in her stay in Britain she discovers that
Communists are blacklisted, even from the auspicious BBC
(5:105), and that the cold war atmosphere in general led
to intellectuals remotely identified with communism to be
considered dangerous (5:131).

Mark Coldridge and his prominent scientist brother
Colin, who defects to the Soviet Union, serve especially
well to demonstrate to Martha the inconsistencies in Communist doctrine and practice, particularly in the anomaly
by which the Communist party simultaneously decried the
Labour party (for being permitted to change society only
insofar as capitalism allowed it to do) and considered it,
after all, as possibly socialist (5:141–42). After Colin's de-
fection, Mark undergoes the same kind of sudden dramatic
conversion by which he sees, among other things, his own
country in a new perspective, as more seriously flawed than
he had realized earlier. But it is suggested that this about-
face results as much from sibling identification as from political conviction (5:174). Similarly, Martha finds herself
wavering: at one point she says she could support neither
America nor communism (5:190), and later is even more
diametrically divided (5:194). Mark also recants: his
"dose" of communism, Martha notes, doesn't affect him
permanently (5:204). Such ex-Communists are derisively
called "revisionists" (5:279), though earlier, when "everyone" had been a Communist, with no petty quarrels distinguishing the various camps, it was forecast that England's Fascist phase—big business backed by the church
and royalty and obeying American bankers—would in time
come into its own (5:558). Joss Cohen, Martha's old friend
from Rhodesia, himself experiences "withdrawal symp-

toms" and is able to return to Africa (5:457). The slogans the various camps of leftists use (5:29, 396) are themselves suggestive of the sterility found in the groups, as are the consistent condescending references to the lower classes, which Martha finds appalling (5:31, 121). Quite early after her arrival in Britain, Martha points out vehemently that it was believed the family would cease to exist when communism came to be established throughout the world, because the party considered the family the source of neurosis, whereas in reality the opposite has occurred: the point of her tearful remarks seems to be that Communist theory removes any consideration of the personal in human relations, which for Martha becomes increasingly more important (5:66–67).

Martha Quest's consistently open interest in sexual expression continues in England as it had in Rhodesia, though now with increasingly little sense of satisfaction in her erotic encounters. Her first lover in England, Jack, is serious only about sex and nothing else; for him sex is a force, not a mere satisfaction (5:58), a force whose laws and control and understanding he passionately seeks out (5:61). Jack also is sexually involved with Joanna, who finds quick and uncomplicated satisfaction all she desires (5:98). When Mark enters her life, Martha finds sex invading her consciousness more than had been true since she arrived in England (5:192, 227, 232). In time they no longer make love (5:284), and Martha, although at this time a mature woman, wonders about the true meaning of the word "sex" (5:380, 470). She discovers, for example, that Jack makes his money through breaking in girls for brothels (5:408–12) and in time she leaves him. For Mark's erotic energy differs from Jack's, with all the words denoting sexual expression lacking in specificity and true meaning (5:470). The increase in sexual deviations such as homosexuality is attributed to a need to protest courageously against the political climate (5:323). An older woman, Margaret, discovers that her third husband is at least partly homosexual, but since she demands companionship more than sex, this is acceptable to her (5:327), and so her home becomes a center devoted to agitation for legalizing sexual inversion (5:362). In time teenage violence becomes the *cause célèbre* for the masses, and homosexuality drops out of the spotlight (5:390), resulting in, among other things, a better erotic relationship between Margaret and her husband (5:398). Martha herself once considers Lesbian activity (5:352), but does not succumb to the temptation. Mark's son, Paul, is involved sexually with Rita, who once accepts an invitation to the home of a sadist (5:548). These, and other deviations that incur the wrath of an increasingly intolerant political order, are the first liberties to fall in the resurgence of puritanism Martha notices in the 1970s, followed by a comparable asceticism in other pleasures (5:567). But since Martha had been aware of such asceticism in her early life, she is better able to understand it, particularly since her mother, in one visit to Martha in London, continues to expose the same reactionary attitude toward sexual expression as when Martha was an adolescent (5:255–56, 271–72). For Martha, however, sex is another of the commitments one makes in life; as she matures and ages, her commitments necessarily change as well, and sex ceases to be the intense, impassioned activity described in the earlier volumes in the series.

The racial tensions found in Rhodesia are, to be sure, different from those encountered in England. But Martha discovers that the attitudes of the "enlightened" Londoners still fall far short of the utopian ideals she had long envisioned. The scare technique of announcing that "the blacks are moving in" a neighborhood is used as effectively in London as in urban centers of this country (5:45). Martha is surprised at her own naïveté in believing that she would be free of the "race thing" when she got to England (5:64), for one of the first things asked her by Phoebe Coldridge, the Labour party worker, is knowledge of the "natives," a term Martha despises (5:81). When Martha sees Jack, her first lover in London, squatting, the act reminds her of a native doing the same thing (5:93). But Martha does become assimilated into London life, and only when her mother visits her do the old colonial attitudes find fervent expression. Mrs. Quest, in her thirty years of life in Africa, had never considered a native African as an equal, had never talked to one as an equal, and in general had maintained prejudices typical of those found in the colonies despite rational evidence to the contrary. Before she leaves for England, she hires a black youth named Steven, who does affect her attitudes; she even catches herself realizing how far she had moved from what she was in considering Steven a person for whom she felt affection (5:244-48, passim). In a mixed gathering in the Coldridge home, Mrs. Quest self-consciously takes a typical colonial stand on the relations between the races in Africa (5:263). When the Maynards, the magistrate and his wife with whom Martha had had many unpleasant experiences in Rhodesia, visit her, Martha sees that no change at all has occurred in their racial attitudes (5:528-29). The mining town in which Rita had grown up in Rhodesia had five thousand whites and one hundred thousand blacks, the latter never seen by young white girls (5:541); her own naïveté is shown in her observation that

> it was a pity that the blacks and the whites couldn't get to know each other as people, because then they would be bound to like each other, people did, when they really knew each other, didn't they? [5:545]

Finally, in the chaotic last days of the world, race riots are described as occurring, but merely as part of the general melee, not as a purely racial matter (5:574), and one of the few survivors of the holocaust is a mixed-blood child (5:609), ironically the closest achieved to Martha's original dream of racial harmony in her "four-gated city" (1:130).

As in the earlier volumes, racial tensions exist regarding Jews. Mark Coldridge, for example, takes upon himself a "burden of guilt about the fate of the Jews in the last war" (5:206). Mrs. Quest almost blurts out the word "Jew" when she meets a young man (5:267), and another person, a young girl, is self-consciously identified as Jewish (5:321, 328). A youth who survived the concentration camps is obsessed with getting to Israel in the years following World

War II; he "became one of the generation who turned their backs on everything traditionally Jewish, the religion, the history, the talent for suffering. . . . His creed was, simply, to fight" (5:438). And Martha finds that she herself uses the language of anti-Semitism, sounding like Goebbels in the process, when she has difficulty writing (5:510, 513). But such emphasis on Jewishness as a form of persecution is considerably less than in the earlier novels in the series, suggesting some slight amelioration in England as contrasted to Rhodesia.

Martha is as self-consciously literary as she was previously. Her extensive reading, the equivalent of a university education, she concludes has taught her merely that no two experts agree (5:213). Mark, as a writer, senses a common cause in Martha, and has her read his first novel, which had received hostile reviews when it was published because it wasn't indignant and filled with protest; it was, instead, a fantasy in which the world was an organism suffering from an incipient boil, i.e., war, and the accepted view at the time (1948) was that war was preventable (5:124–25). Although Mark was at first too discouraged to write another novel, he does receive a visit from a literary agent who tries to persuade him that his next book ought to be concerned more with the "eternal truths" within man, which, Mrs. Lessing observes, is an indication that "hard times are on the way" in England; hence Mark's novel was published several years too early (5:131–32). When Mark does write a short version about his planned desert refuge-city in Africa, Martha reads it with great interest (5:134–35). When the book based on this short account is completed, Martha senses the similarity of emotional tone it has with Thomas Stern's wildly paranoid manuscript which she has been preserving (5:176). Mark considers a new novel but is warned that the "proletarian novel" so loved by the Communist movement is dead, even though this is what he begins (5:177–78). No Communist, it was believed, could have written Mark's *A City in the Desert*; the author must have changed his political views (5:203). Suddenly, though, after years of being ostracized, Mark is besieged with requests for articles and reviews (5:203) as well as for another book (5:232–33), and his visionary book even gets published in the United States, where it is welcomed by science-fiction enthusiasts (5:284). Martha, however, aside from occasional letters, does no writing of her own; her preference is for passive evaluation of Mark's books, or science-fiction thrillers by Jimmy Woods, another friend. Mark writes a play, successfully produced; he prepares another novel, a short one identified with anti-Semitism, which is received indifferently by the press (5:438–39). Furthermore, it becomes the fashion to read works of fiction in terms of their autobiographical elements (5:450), as offensive to Mark as to Mrs. Lessing herself. Jimmy Woods's extensive collection of books on the occult, used for subjects for his science-fiction novels, are borrowed by Martha to satisfy her intense curiosity about strange, new subjects (5:488–89).

But as the world changes radically in the 1960s, both Mark and Martha find that imminent catastrophe requires radically altered adaptations in their thinking, and necessarily as well in their response to reading and other forms of creativity. Thomas Stern's impassioned, mad manuscript is read by and commented on by Mark (5:489–90), and Martha undergoes the same kind of frantic scribbling identified with greatest candor and detail in Mrs. Lessing's *The Golden Notebook*, discussed in the next chapter. Martha is as concerned as Anna Wulf (the protagonist of *The Golden Notebook*) with getting as much on paper as possible before it vanishes forever; her excessive self-pity and hysteria, described in detail (5:509–24, passim), is given in surrealistic terms and with Martha said to succumb to the Devil and his foul desires. The paranoia this reflects is comparable to stages in Lynda's thinking, to be touched on below. For Mark, though, his apocalyptic writings bring him to the attention of a wealthy American industrialist who finances his plan to build an ideal city in Africa (5:551–52). Hence writing and reading become, not a form of therapy as Mrs. Lessing suggests is the case in *The Golden Notebook*, but a final apocalyptic means of sensing the dissolution of civilization, and, in Mark's case, of enabling him to build his futile refuge from catastrophe in the desert. Neither Mark's active involvement in writing, nor Martha's passive absorption of the ideas to be found in Mark's books and elsewhere, can effectively prepare them for total annihilation when it comes.

Far more than in any of her other books except *The Golden Notebook*, Mrs. Lessing is concerned in *The Four-Gated City* with mental imbalance and lack of equilibrium. Martha Quest increasingly recognizes the limitations of normal reasoning as a means of bringing order out of disorder. Martha's initial sensing herself to be an outsider in London (5:21) soon changes to a feeling of alienation from a great many of the realities of her new world. Martha has lapses of memory (5:39, 221), and once deliberately gives a wrong name when asked her identity (5:17). A sense of *déjà vu* hits her on occasion (5:149, 309, 368), clearly related to Martha's persistent sense of not knowing her identity, of seeing herself as split. Initially upon arriving in England she is not sure she is Martha or Matty (5:5), and frequently thereafter the same tension is felt (5:132, 216, 219, 226–27, 310, 337). But Lynda also reflects a schizophrenic condition, among other psychotic or neurotic tendencies, a fact that enables the two women to identify with each other (e.g., 5:468–69, 473–74), and especially for Martha to learn of hidden psychic realms such as extrasensory perception. Martha's intensive reading in Freud and Jung (5:212) prepares her for her discoveries of psychic phenomena. Lynda herself, so completely unbalanced as to be described as a "psychological cripple," spends a month by herself in the basement, a kind of symbolic descent into hell (5:498). In one of the "documents" concluding the novel proper, the possibilities of telepathy are described in detail by Lynda's daughter, noting especially what such a talent had cost Lynda in health and sanity (5:585, 587).

Though dreams are not emphasized in this novel as much as in the next to be discussed, they still demonstrate for Martha a remarkable sense of her choices in life and, on occasion, become themselves nightmarish visions of the world to come. She still dreams of Africa (e.g., 5:220), but more often than not her dream life is occupied with visions of death (5:304), fantasy (5:311), the reek of excrement spoiling a lovely vista (5:478–79), apocalyptic visions of a future world in which normal human traits and features are perverted (5:480–82), surrealistic fantasies (5:513–14), hell (5:522) and an old friend seducing Mark (5:538). Lynda also has fantastic visions and dreams, one notable nightmare being a series of glimpses of a poisoned England (5:536–37). But Martha, who had once dreamed of the same ideal city serving as the novel's title (5:206), increasingly wonders whether it is possible to control one's dreams (5:484), again an allusion to the kind of extraordinary sensory acuteness she shares with Lynda. And one prime result of such mental or extramental processes is Martha's keen awareness of the cataclysmic future awaiting her and the world around her.

Most of Mrs. Lessing's female protagonists are concerned with a self-conscious awareness of either being free or lacking freedom, and Martha Quest, as we have already seen, is especially concerned with liberating herself from the conformist institutions around her. In *The Four-Gated City* this emphasis remains but is somewhat altered. Immediately after her arrival in London, Martha gloats in her newfound freedom, a kind she had never known previously (5:4–5). But only Jack, her first lover in London, would allow her to remain free and rootless (5:38). On those rare occasions when she thinks of her daughter, left behind in Rhodesia, Martha says she had set her free (5:66). When Mark suggests the job that Martha eventually keeps for twenty years, she recognizes that "for the first time since she came to London, she was unfree" (5:89). On occasion the meaning of the word "freedom" is debated, but rarely with any agreement possible (5:126, 351). When Rita, the daughter of Martha's friend Maisie in Rhodesia, comes to England, Martha is struck again by the seeming meaninglessness of the word (5:543, 544, 547). Finally, in the apocalyptic portion of the novel, reference is made to a pilot choosing "freedom" by crashing into England with a nuclear bomb aboard his plane, thus effectively wiping out the country (5:599). Hence when Martha and Lynda are compared to machines of various sorts (5:476), their lack of freedom is implied as much as the resurgence of Ludditism later on (5:569) suggests an unwillingness to be governed by machines; in both cases "freedom," however poorly defined, serves as a corrective to feelings of mass conformity and coerced behavior increasingly accepted by a passive populace (5:443, 567–68). As Mark's stepdaughter says toward the end of the novel, "we were slowly driving ourselves mad" (5:576) and utterly helpless (5:578). Martha, in one of the last statements she makes before dying, senses a "sweet high loveliness somewhere . . . with a bright promise. Of what? Love? Joy?" (5:604), and Mark, just before his death, says, "We have no enemy. The human race is united at last. . . . We are all brothers now" (5:612). This combination is suggestive of the idyllic future envisioned in the words of Schiller used for the final movement of Beethoven's Ninth Symphony; Mrs. Lessing seems to be equivocal about the chances of such an ideal world of love and brotherliness ever actually being achieved, for the culminating lines of the book are unrelievedly filled with accounts of death and holocaust. Certainly a mutation of humanity is suggested as well as psychic acuteness not presently possessed by mankind; and Mrs. Lessing seems personally sure that mankind will survive the cataclysm presently being experienced.[9]

One cannot deny that *The Four-Gated City* is too diffuse, too long, and filled with fascinating but undeveloped ideas and plot-strands. But as a whole it is a chilling culmination to the series which Mrs. Lessing began as an account of a young girl growing up in colonial Africa. Although she calls the book a *Bildungsroman*, this book differs from many books of that genre in that far more than the protagonist's maturing years are described. Further, since Martha is a passive, not an active, force in the novel, she seems at times almost as if more was altered than her place of residence between volumes from four and five in the series. Frederick P. W. McDowell has acutely observed that the chief defect of the book is its diffuseness, its sharp contrast between the scenes of horror in contemporary England and the cataclysmic vision which ends the book.[10] All in all, however, the book is a most striking fictional experiment—and experience—and fully demonstrates Mrs. Lessing's continuing goal for the series: "a study of the individual conscience in its relations with the collective." As such, it is a rich, disturbing portent of mankind's certain destiny if immediate alterations in his behavior and thinking are not forthcoming. Indeed, the book demands a total assimilation into our life if we are to be the inheritors of tomorrow.

4

The Golden Notebook

Mrs. Lessing's protagonists, as intelligent, sensitive women in the midst of racial and political turmoil, necessarily find two areas, the racial and political, occupying much of their thought and activity, and as a corollary to this preoccupation, they become increasingly aware of their status in an essentially masculine world. While Martha Quest is not "emancipated" in the trite and stereotyped sense (i.e., so concerned with sexual equality that it becomes a morbid, dehumanizing obsession blocking out all other considerations), she does manifest such a degree of personal integrity that she cannot look passively on injustice and prejudice, just as her acuteness of perspective gives her a far more coherent method of evaluating the conflict between her own generation and that of her parents than is true of most adolescents and young adults. But Martha Quest, in some ways, seems an apprenticeship-effort for the creation of Anna Freeman Wulf, Mrs. Lessing's protagonist in *The Golden Notebook* and by far one of the most consciously self-critical and analytical women in modern fiction.

Unlike Martha, though, Anna senses the incoherence in her life to such a degree that she attempts to compartmentalize it, thus giving the reader individual glimpses of several distinct and unique sides to Anna's psyche. Anna's method in detailing her own gradual mental and psychological disintegration takes the form of four separate notebooks in which she systematically recounts the events and thoughts in four different time spans or "moods" of her life: a black notebook (for the events in "black" Africa), a red notebook (for her time as a Communist), a yellow notebook (a fictionalized effort to see herself in perspective), and a blue notebook (primarily a factual diary-account of her life). These are in turn succeeded and superseded by another notebook, the golden one of the novel's title.

Thus while Anna, like her predecessors in Mrs. Lessing's fiction, finds racial and political concerns forcing a personal commitment, each is displaced by a successive commitment; only when the commitment that seems also to be Mrs. Lessing's is recognized and adopted—the commitment to individual artistic expression, such as through writing—does Anna achieve emotional and personal equilibrium. Thereafter she does not lose her concern for idealistic theory and practice, but she rechannels these drives into personally satisfying public forms; no longer, for instance, does she work surreptitiously and frustratingly for communism, but instead turns to more publicly acceptable political expression, to the British Labour party. And by turning from a private to a public use of language, she eliminates the incoherence in her personal emotional life.

Mrs. Lessing had suggested some of the same character types and emphases found in *The Golden Notebook* in a play produced at the Royal Court Theatre in 1958, *Each His Own Wilderness*. A brief examination of this play, I believe, can help lead to a greater understanding of the later novel. Two middle-aged women named Myra and Milly, both evidently divorced or widowed, work with high dedication in their particular social and political realms, but both experience difficulty in achieving harmonious relationships with their respective sons, who are alike in reflecting a malaise about life and an indifference toward the issues that concern their mothers so deeply. Not only is a conflict of generations present, but also a gulf that is never satisfactorily breached: the mothers, as fairly typical women of the 1950s, want their children to make up their own minds about life, while the sons long for a serene, settled way of life. Tony, Myra's son, for example, says to her,

I've spent a good part of what are known as my forma-
tive years listening to the conversation of the mature.
You set my teeth on edge. You're corrupt, you're sloppy
and corrupt. I'm waiting for the moment when you put
your foot down about something and say you've had
enough. But you never do. All you do is watch things —
with interest.[1]

Another statement, the source of the play's title, concerns
the generation of Tony's mother and the special kind of
world it has created for his generation:

Do you know what you've created, you and your lot?
What a vision it is! A house for every family. . . . A
house full of clean, well-fed people, and not one of them
ever understands one word anyone else says. Everybody
a kind of wilderness surrounded by barbed wire shouting
across the defences into the other wilderness and never
getting an answer back. That's socialism. I suppose it's
progress. Why not. . . . To every man his front door
and his front door key. To each his own wilderness.[2]

Much of the play concerns Tony's gradual estrangement
from his mother, as he first discovers her sacrifice in aiding
his education and Myra's ultimately leaving the house to
her son, discouraged as she is at her sense of having wasted
her life. For she has been promiscuous, she has, really, little
to show (both in life and in her son) for her efforts, and
she is far more dedicated as a human being than her son.
Perhaps the trouble, in a word, is that she believes too much
and he believes nothing.

In 1962, another play, *Play with a Tiger* (also written in
1958), was produced in the Comedy Theatre in London,
and is somewhat more explicit in its relationship to *The
Golden Notebook*. This play, whose title gives the novel
one of its central symbolic motifs,[3] again presents two people in an impassioned dialogue, an intellectual heroine and
her younger American lover. The two are involved in the
same kind of love-hate relationship Anna and Saul Green,

the younger American writer with whom she for a time lives, have in *The Golden Notebook*; both are attracted to the other, but both realize the necessity of overcoming the other or of being overcome. While dramatically this play is no more satisfying than the other discussed,[4] it does show an organic and thematic similarity to the novel itself, and serves as a kind of trying-out of some of the character relationships and incidents of the novel.

Even without relying too heavily upon these earlier plays as possible sources for *The Golden Notebook*, one can easily see affinities between Mrs. Lessing's own life and the characters and emphases of the novel. Instead, one complaint Mrs. Lessing has continually voiced since the novel's publication has been the tendency of reviewers and critics to confuse the fictional protagonist and the author herself. In an interview in the *Queen*, a British magazine, Mrs. Lessing said she was "appalled" at the "frivolity" and "amateurishness" of the reviews, since they were mostly interested in seeing an alleged Marxist or sexual orientation for the novel as a whole, or, worse, in seeing the book on the "gossip-column" level,[5] with the author perfectly equated with the heroine. Indeed, as Mrs. Lessing said in another interview, some critics tried to turn the book into "The Confessions of Doris Lessing." [6] And in a letter, Mrs. Lessing goes even further by saying that

> this autobiographical approach by critics is a very bad and indeed a very frivolous one. . . . Like every other writer, my novels are a mixture of straight (as far as anything can be) autobiography, and creation. . . . A young lady came to interview me from the Observor [*sic*] recently, and I said: Well at least they can't say *Landlocked* is autobiographical. Her reply was: But of course they say it is. "Why?" I ask. Because it is so convincing, she replies.
>
> I thought it was the job of a writer to make things convincing.
>
> This annoys me not because it is personally annoying, but because it means people don't read what I've written

in the right way. The right way to read a novel is as if its [*sic*] a thing by itself, with its own laws, with due attention to its shape, not with reference back to possible autobiographical incidents.[7]

One might go even further to say that *The Golden Notebook*, a book about a woman with a writer's block, could scarcely be the story of Mrs. Lessing herself, since she obviously has no writer's block. Hence one must consider the book not so much as an autobiographical or confessional novel, but more as a highly detailed examination of the forces which have gone into the complicated life of a real person who has some parallel characteristics with her fictional protagonist.

Mrs. Lessing has been keenly aware of the emphasis in twentieth-century literature on the artist's sensibility, and has singled out Thomas Mann as having devoted his entire life to an examination of this theme. But Mrs. Lessing says she has a "kind of hostility to the idea that an artist's sensibility should represent everyone," and that she wonders what, if anything, one could say about the theme after Mann's exhaustive examination. The "logical next step," she says, is that of a writer who cannot write. But this writer's block should result from "good intellectual reasons" such as political involvement; thus a development of such reasons, individually good as they are, would show how destructive they become when they lead to artistic inertia. In Anna Freeman Wulf, the protagonist of *The Golden Notebook*, Mrs. Lessing says, such a destructive emphasis causes the excessive "aggression, madness, cruelty, mixed up with love, kindness, and everything" that we find in the novel. "Not until the cruelty and aggression come out and are acknowledged," Mrs. Lessing adds, can Anna "start creating again." The writer's block itself, Mrs. Lessing says, is a way of saying something "about a certain way of looking at the world," a way which while not wholly Marxist is based in part on this political philosophy and such kinds of education as those assuming that "everything is of the best, justice will prevail, that human beings are equal, that if we try hard enough, society is going to become perfect, that people are fundamentally good." Thus *The Golden Notebook* is a novel about "certain political and sexual attitudes, that have force now; it is an attempt to explain them, to objectivise them, to set them in relation with each other. So in a way it is a social novel." [8]

More integrally important than the immediate stimulus for this novel, though, is Mrs. Lessing's deep concern over form. She has said that its "meaning is in the shape," [9] and that the particular shape was chosen because she "wanted to write a short formal novel which would enclose the rest in order to suggest what I think a great many writers feel about the formal novel; namely, that it's not doing its job any more. So I thought that the only way to do this would be to write the short formal novel and put in the experience it came out of, showing how ridiculous the formal novel is when it can't say a damned thing. . . . So I put in the short formal novel and *all this*." [10] Indeed, so insistent was Mrs. Lessing in setting this short novel (i.e., the passages labeled "Free Women" taken collectively) apart from the rest of the book that it is even set in a different typeface from the rest of the novel—"in a rather old-fashioned print, with rather flowery chapter headings, to suggest that this kind of novel is old-fashioned." [11] Shape is, moreover, an integral part of the rest of the novel, since Mrs. Lessing says she "split up the rest into four parts to express a split person. I felt that if the artist's sensibility is to be equated with the sensibility of the educated person, then it is logical to use different styles to express different kinds of people. . . . Also this particular form enabled me to say things about time, about memory—which interests me very much; what we choose to remember—about the human personality because a personality is very much what is remembered. . . . If I had used a conventional style, the old-fashioned novel . . . I would not have been able to do this kind of playing with time, memory and the balancing of people." [12] And elsewhere she has said that *The Golden Notebook* was a "very highly structured book, carefully planned. The point of that book was the relation of its parts to each other." [13]

Finally, Mrs. Lessing, for the original British edition of *The Golden Notebook,* made this statement (quoted from the book jacket):

> About five years ago I found myself thinking about the novel most writers now are tempted to write at some time or another—about the problems of a writer, about the artistic sensibility. I saw no point in writing this again: it has been done too often; it has been one of the major themes of the novel in our time. Yet, having decided not to write it, I continued to think about it, and about the reasons why artists have to combat various kinds of narcissism. I found that if it were to be written at all, the subject should be, not a practising artist, but an artist with some kind of a block which prevented him or her from creating. In describing the reasons for the block, I would also be making the criticism I wanted to make about our society. I would be describing a disgust and self-division which afflicts people now, and not only artists.
>
> Simultaneously I was working out another book, a book of literary criticism, which I would write not as a critic, but as practising writer, using various literary styles, in such a way that the shape of the book would provide the criticism. Since I hold that criticism of literature is a criticism and judgement of life, this book would say what I wanted to say about life; it would make, implicitly, a statement about what Marxists call alienation.
>
> Thinking about these two books, I understood suddenly they were not two books but one; they were fusing together in my mind. I understood that the shape of this book should be enclosed and claustrophobic—so narcissistic that the subject matter must break through the form.
>
> This novel, then, is an attempt to break a form; to break certain forms of consciousness and go beyond them.

Quoting Mrs. Lessing's statements of intention regarding *The Golden Notebook* at such length, then, ought to indicate the degree to which her accomplishment in the novel is deliberate and self-consciously one in which both form and content are necessarily closely linked—perhaps more so than in most novels of our or any time—and that the novel is considerably more than mere self-confessional.

A brief statement about the exact ordering of the materials in *The Golden Notebook* would not, perhaps, be wholly out of place here. All four of the major notebooks are written in the first person, and cover roughly the years from 1950 to 1957, with the fifth notebook (the golden one) describing only events during 1957, the year of its composition, and with Anna's one successful novel, *Frontiers of War*, having been published during or shortly after World War II. There are also five sections labeled "Free Women," written in the third person and, as we discover toward the end of the entire novel, purportedly written by Anna. These "Free Women" passages also describe events during the last year covered by the notebooks, 1957. The book opens with the first of the "Free Women" sections, followed by the four notebooks, in succession, black, red, yellow, and blue, with this pattern repeated four times and with the individual notebook sections varying from one page to some eighty pages in length. After the fourth repeating of this pattern comes the section based on Anna's last, the golden, notebook, and with the entire novel then concluded with a final "Free Women" episode.

But since the "Free Women" passages (comprising the "short formal novel" mentioned earlier) are an attempt at describing the thoughts and activities of an alter ego of Anna's, there are of necessity a number of inconsistencies in detail. Most obvious of these is the choice of endings: if we are to believe the final notebook entry, Anna, after she is given the first sentence of a novel by her young American lover, starts to write the first of the "Free Women" passages, while the ending of the final "Free Women" section presents Ella, Anna's alter ego, planning to "join the Labour Party and teach a night-class twice a week for delinquent kids." [14] Furthermore, Tommy, Anna's son, is described in the opening "Free Women" section as being twenty years old in 1957 (p. 13) and seventeen years old in a notebook purporting to describe events in 1950 (p.

197); he later gets married, according to the notebooks (p. 468), or travels to Sicily with his father's wife (p. 554). While attempts at resolving such inconsistencies must ultimately be impossible, they seem to be part of the attempt on Anna's part to reflect and emphasize certain parts of life, not to mirror them perfectly in all respects. Thus one can read the "Free Women" sections as a kind of coda or variation on the themes emphasized in the notebooks, with Anna's controlled attempts at writing being the means by which she (but not necessarily her fictional alter ego) can achieve both a meaningful relationship with other people and an ordered personal identity. As a whole, then, these "Free Women" passages are a fictionalized effort by Anna to see herself in perspective, not a point-by-point parallel to her own life, and as such, their organic relationship to the story of Anna Wulf herself becomes clearer.

As has already been suggested, there is a pervasive awareness of the complex and constantly simmering racial struggle in central colonial Africa running throughout most of the writing of Doris Lessing. Even in those works, like *The Golden Notebook*, which are not directly set in Africa, there is a constant presence of Africa noticeable in many subtle but inescapable references and emphases. As was quoted earlier, Doris Lessing has said that she was

brought up in Central Africa, which means that I was a member of the white minority, pitted against a black majority that was abominably treated and still is. I was the daughter of a white farmer who, although he was a very poor man in terms of what he was brought up to expect, could always get loans from the Land Bank which kept him. (I won't say that my father liked what was going on; he didn't.) But he employed anywhere from fifty to one hundred working blacks. An adult black earned twelve shillings a month, rather less than two dollars, and his food was rationed to corn meal and beans and peanuts and a pound of meat per week. It was all grossly unfair, and it's only a part of a larger picture of inequity.[15]

So explicit has Mrs. Lessing been in citing this injustice in detail, particularly (but not exclusively) in those works specifically concerned with Africa, that after a return trip in 1956 to Southern Rhodesia and South Africa, she found herself in the company of many of her friends in "being prohibited," as she has called it, that is, in being permanently exiled from the country in which she was raised. Thus she was not among those who were surprised at the dissolution of the Central African Federation in 1963, following a span of only a decade in which "the politics of partnership" was discarded as unworkable.[16]

Anna's own constant thinking about the African situation most often takes the form of entries in the black notebook, in which she describes memories and her own innermost thoughts and convictions about the black-white struggle. Toward the end of the black notebook entries, she describes a dream she has had, a recurring dream, about the individuals she had previously known in Africa. This particular entry contains a series of news items, every one of which refers to "violence, death, rioting, hatred, in some part of Africa" (p. 449). Anna dreams that a television film is to be made about the people she had known at the Mashopi Hotel in the colony. Although the director tells Anna in the dream that the script would be "exactly what [she] would have written [herself]," she soon discovers that his choice of shots and timing changes the "story" as she recalls it, that she no longer recognizes the lines spoken or even the relationships described, and that the technicians and cameramen, all black, alter the cameras into machine guns. The director defends his version of the incident because "it doesn't matter what we film, provided we film something" (p. 450). In short, Anna no longer remembers the "real" past, and cannot say exactly why the version being filmed is "wrong."

Anna also recalls in her notebook entries several Africans she has met and has talked with in an earlier day. Of these, Tom Mathlong and Charlie Themba are most prominent. Tom Mathlong especially becomes a kind of conscience for Anna, and even when not present except in her thoughts, his influence is pervasive and strong. When, for example, she and her friends, Marion and Tommy, express an interest in African nationalism, she tells them, first, that they must "stop this pretence of caring about African nationalism," and that they "both know quite well it's nonsense" (p. 436). She then immediately ponders,

> Well, what would Tom Mathlong say? She imagined herself sitting across the table in a cafe with Tom Mathlong telling him about Marion and Tommy. He would listen and say: "Anna, you tell me why these two people have chosen to work for African liberation? And why should I care about their motives?" But then he would laugh. Yes. Anna could hear his laugh, deep, full, shaken out of his stomach. Yes. He would put his hands on his knees and laugh, then shake his head and say: "My dear Anna, I wish we had your problems." [P. 436]

Indeed, Mathlong is a kind of saint, for he combines not only the idealism of the Communist party members mentioned above, but also an awareness of the ultimate rightness of his cause. He sees, in a word, not only the heights to which man's sense of ethicality can raise him, but also that sense of ethicality in perspective, in relation to those more sordid areas of life such as the inexorably slow progress visible in racial terms at any one moment. And although Anna, after pondering the meaning of the word, again says that Tom is a saint—"an ascetic, but not a neurotic one" (p. 440)—she recognizes, from his stoical acceptance of the inevitability of years in prison because of his nationalistic efforts, the degree to which he is perhaps too ideal for an imperfect world.

By contrast with Tom Mathlong, Charlie Themba, the other native discussed in detail in *The Golden Notebook*, demonstrates an opposite kind of character, one more approximating the opportunistic superiority of the whites in colonial Africa. No racial exclusiveness for him; he longs instead for political power as a means of personal aggrandizement and promotion. He had shown a similar high-mindedness to that of Mathlong's but ultimately becomes distrusted by his fellow natives. Anna describes Themba as a trade union leader,[17] "violent and passionate and quarrelsome and loyal" (p. 441), and recently "cracked up" because of the pressure of politics—"full of intrigue and jealousness and spite." Themba, evidently paranoid and even psychotic, believes that Mathlong and others are intriguing against him, so he begins writing bitter, fantastic letters to people like Anna who know him. These hysterical and incoherent communications show the degree to which a right-minded person, as a result of psychological and social pressures, loses not only his idealism but also his psychic balance.

But if Tom Mathlong represents the consistently ethical and trustworthy extreme, with Charlie Themba moving from that extreme toward one of opportunism and mental chaos, there is yet another type of native to be mentioned, the opposite extreme from Tom Mathlong. While this type is not singled out and named as an individual, he is described in terms generically applicable to purely opportunistic politicians the world around: "he's bombastic and rabble-rousing and he drinks and he whores around. He'll probably be the first Prime Minister—he has all the qualities—the common touch, you know" (p. 440).

These complicated and involved examples of the racial situation in Rhodesia show more than anything else the kind of commitment, admittedly a frustrating, futile one, that enlightened individuals like Anna Wulf dedicate themselves to during their African years. But just as the various natives described range from purely idealistic to purely opportunistic, so the whites too react in varying ways to the racial situation. Anna and others admit the wrongness of *apartheid* (even though this term is not used in the novel), but their ineffectual attempts at remedying the situation cause some to be so disillusioned that they give up, while others become cynically a part of the dominant power structure. As with both Mrs. Lessing herself and her earlier fictional creation, Martha Quest, Anna finds the frustrations and pressures too great to endure without signs of victory, so another commitment is made: to political action, particularly to Communist party activity.

In common with many other British and American in-tellectuals in the 1930s and early 1940s, Doris Lessing be-came a Communist as a result of sincere optimistic desires to see the world improved and to have the injustices of a supposedly inhuman competitive system of values elimi-nated. To a great extent, her decision to become a Com-munist appears now as naïve as many other youthful en-thusiasms or commitments. She has said, for instance,

> when I became a communist, emotionally if not organi-zationally, in 1942, my picture of socialism as developed in the Soviet Union was, to say the least, inaccurate. But after fifteen years of uncomfortable adjustment to real-ity I still find myself in the possession of an optimism about the future obviously considered jejune by anyone under the age of thirty. . . . Perhaps it is that the result of having been a communist is to be a humanist.[18]

For the writer, uniquely equipped to communicate the po-litical tensions of an era, has as his "point of rest" his

> recognition of man, the responsive individual, voluntar-ily submitting his will to the collective, but never finally; and insisting on making his own personal and private judgements before every act of submission.[19]

Thus the same tension between the individual sense of re-sponsibility and the collective emphasis on conformist thinking which has led so many idealists out of the party they considered a panacea for the world's economic and so-cial ills is responsible for Mrs. Lessing's own disenchant-ment after some years' allegiance to the Communist party.

This allegiance, though, did not suddenly cease as if a radical experience such as a conversion had occurred. She has said that she

> decided to leave the party a good time before I finally left it. I didn't leave it when I decided to, because there was a general exodus, much publicized, from the British Party then, and the journalists were waiting for yet an-other renegade to publish his, her complaints against the C.P. [Communist Party]. To quote another old commu-

nist: "I find it nauseating when people who have been in the Party ten, twenty years, stagger out shouting and screaming as if they've been raped against their will." I left it because the gap between my own attitudes and those of the party widened all the time. There was no particular event or moment. The 20th Congress [in February, 1956, at which Khrushchev denounced Stalin] shocked me, not because of the "revelations" but because I thought the "revelations" were long overdue, pitifully and feebly put forth, and no one really tried to explain or understand what had happened.[20]

It is in Anna Wulf that Mrs. Lessing's subtle shifting of loyalty to communism is best illustrated, not only because of the later date of composition of *The Golden Notebook*, but also because of the fuller character portrayal we have of Anna than of earlier characters. Indeed, since *The Golden Notebook* is concerned most directly with the later stages in the political metamorphosis of Anna Wulf, we are given far more to support a person's leaving the party than his joining it. Anna once reflects that intelligent Communists believe the party "has been saddled with a group of dead bureaucrats who run it, and that the real work gets done in spite of the centre" (p. 137). Hence she and most other Communists mentioned in the book suffer a profound disillusionment, perhaps best illustrated by the bitter comment by Maryrose, a young Communist Anna had known in Africa: "Only a few months ago we believed that the world was going to change and everything was going to be beautiful and now we know it won't" (p. 117). And Anna herself, in one of her recurring dreams, tells about one particularly apocalyptic vision she has in which she foresees an end to the Communist system, at the very least for herself personally (pp. 256–57).

An end to communism, though, will result less from wishful dreaming than from the weight of the party's own weaknesses—none of which, really, have anything to do with party doctrine per se so much as the increasing bureaucratization and narrowness of thinking Anna sees aound her.

Thus the Communists portrayed in *The Golden Notebook* are consistently either those like Anna and Maryrose, disillusioned and despondent, or like Willi Rodde, who becomes part of the East German bureaucracy after the war; there seems to be no middle ground, such as impassioned dedication to the Communist cause, as can be found on occasion in Mrs. Lessing's earlier books.

Anna in particular notices with increasing distaste and disgust the official party falsification of truth whenever it seems expedient. Because of her work for John Butte, a Communist publisher, she is in a unique position to see at firsthand the exact ways in which such falsification takes place; indeed, it is the world of publishing that first interests her in joining the Communist party. But Anna soon finds out that the "truth" is not a very highly prized commodity in Communist publishing. She, as an editor, is given a novel by a faithful party member to consider for publication, which she evaluates as follows:

> This novel touches reality at no point at all. (Jack described it as "communist cloud-cuckoo spit.") It is, however, a very accurate recreation of the self-deceptive myths of the Communist Party at this particular time; and I have read it in about fifty shapes or guises during the last year. I say: "you know quite well this is a very bad book.". . . He [Butte] now remarks: "It's no masterpiece . . . but it's a good book, I think.". . . I will challenge him, and he will argue. The end will be the same, because the decision has already been taken. The book will be published. People in the Party with any discrimination will be even more ashamed because of the steadily debasing values of the Party; the *Daily Worker* will praise it. [P. 296]

After Butte, exasperated, says, "Publish and be damned!", Anna says,

> What you've said sums up everything that is wrong with the Party. It's a crystallization of the intellectual rottenness of the Party that the cry of nineteenth-century hu-

manism, courage against odds, truth against lies, should
be used now to defend the publication of a lousy lying
book by a communist firm which will risk nothing at all
by publishing it, not even a reputation for integrity.
[P. 297]

But Anna, herself sufficiently a person with integrity to admit the necessity of accepting her changing political views,
can only protest; she cannot change the situation. For a
time, though, she is temporarily recharged with enthusiasm
and hope for the party, following the death of Stalin on
March 5, 1953. Anna for a time believes that there is again
a chance for a meaningful allegiance to communism. But
the resurgence of hope does not last long; after she has
been out of the party for over a year, she is invited back for
a meeting at which the bureaucracy is supposedly to be re-
moved and the party in Britain revitalized, "without the
deadly loyalty to Moscow and the obligation to tell lies"
(p. 382). But less than a year later, at another meeting, she
realizes that she has accomplished nothing in all the "frenzied political activity" in which she has been involved. In
short, Anna's renewed sense of purpose in the Communist
party is short-lived, for she discovers that the situation she
had sensed earlier, and which led her to her leaving the
party, has not really changed at all.

Although Anna indicates at various times her reasons for
leaving the party—its jargon, its dishonesty, its pettiness,
and so on—she does specify in one passage in more detail
her exact reasons for both becoming a Communist and for
leaving the party. Jack, another party member, comments
that society today is complex and technical that no one person can effectively understand it all. Anna answers him:

"Alienation. Being split. It's the moral side, so to speak,
of the communist message. And suddenly you shrug your
shoulders and say because the mechanical basis of our
lives is getting complicated, we must be content to not
even try to understand things as a whole?" And now I
see his face has put on a stubborn closed look that reminds me of John Butte's: and he looks angry. He says:
"Not being split, it's not a question of imaginatively un-

derstanding everthing that goes on. Or trying to. It means doing one's work as well as possible, and being a good person." I say: "That's treachery." "To what?" "To humanism." He thinks and says: "The idea of humanism will change like everything else." I say: "Then it will become something else. But humanism stands for the whole person, the whole individual, striving to become as conscious and responsible as possible about everything in the universe. But now you sit there, quite calmly, and as a humanist you say that due to the complexity of scientific achievement the human being must never expect to be whole, he must always be fragmented." [Pp. 307–8]

Her sense of this fragmentation is such as to demand of her a more coherent, a more unifying life than has been possible through dedication to communism. Although party membership and activity can be a meaningful commitment, Anna discovers that it is too limited a commitment, too narrow in its rewards and too dishonest in its demands upon the individual, to remain for long the kind of commitment she needs for her own life. Again, she must move on to a further level of commitment, that of an open and free acknowledgement of her sexual nature, before she is able to move to what I believe is her ultimate and most lasting commitment, to verbal communication through writing for a public audience.

As Anna Wulf continues in her process of attempting to bring meaning into the chaos of her life, we see how she gradually but perceptibly moves from a purely objective area of concern (the racial), to an area with both objective theory and personal application (the political), and now to the more wholly subjective. That is, as an enlightened, liberal white, Anna is scarcely as involved in the fight for racial justice as, say, Tom Mathlong; as a sensitive, intelligent, and idealistic young woman, she cannot assimilate the inconsistencies and pettiness of communism; and now, we see another area of commitment in Anna's life, that collectively concerned with her views on sex and marriage, and, concurrently, her need of psychoanalytic counselling. This considerably more subjective commitment requires of Anna a correspondingly greater degree of insight into her own psyche and personality, as well as a frank admission of the exact kind of woman she is.

As we first meet Anna and see her in her milieu, we notice the extent to which she and her friend, Molly, seem conventionally "emancipated," particularly in the areas of sexual morality and their ability to move freely through what is always an explicitly masculine world. The term they use to refer to themselves, "free women," is itself the overall title for the short novel Anna writes about her alter ego, and thus it is no surprise that the concept of freedom occurs frequently in *The Golden Notebook*. But the concept itself changes as Anna step-by-step becomes more fully aware of her identity. Molly's statement early in the novel, "we're a completely new type of woman" (p. 10), is fairly typical of the self-conscious "emancipation" the two women adopt. Anna asks a bit later, "if we lead what is known as free lives, that is, lives like men, why shouldn't we use the same language?" Molly replies, "Because we aren't the same. That is the point." Anna's retort to this posits the essential contrast between the sexes evident throughout the book: "Men. Women. Bound. Free. Good. Bad. Yes. No. Capitalism. Socialism. Sex. Love." (p. 43). Despite this, Anna senses that women's "loyalties are always to men, and not to women" (p. 46); she painfully realizes she is approaching middle age, and recalls that when she was younger, twenty-three or so, she suffered "from a terror of being trapped and tamed by domesticity" (p. 114–15). Now, though, she realizes the extent to which she is lonely. Molly reminds her in these terms of her loneliness:

> You choose to be alone rather than to get married for the sake of not being lonely. . . . You're afraid of writing what you think about life, because you might find yourself in an exposed position, you might expose yourself, you might be alone. [P. 39]

And later, when Anna canvasses for the Communist party, she notices the many lonely women who long for an audience for their personal problems, "going mad quietly by themselves, in spite of husband and children or rather because of them" (p. 146). Much later, when Anna leaves her lover (as described in the final "Free Women" section), she recognizes the price she must pay for being as free and independent and intelligent as she is: "that will be my epitaph. Here lies Anna Wulf, who was always too intelligent. She let them go" (P. 562). For the toughness Anna so proudly claims for herself is seen to be more attitude than actuality, as when she tells Molly about the kind of life the two are living:

> Both of us are dedicated to the proposition that we're tough. . . . A marriage breaks up, well, we say, our marriage was a failure, too bad. A man ditches us—too bad we say, it's not important. We bring up kids without men—nothing to it, we say, we can cope. We spend years in the communist party and then we say, well, well, we made a mistake, too bad. . . . Well don't you think it's at least possible that things can happen to us so bad that we don't ever get over them? . . . Why do our lot never admit failure? Never. It might be better for us if we did. And it's not only love and men. Why can't we say something like this—we are people, because of the accident of how we were situated in history, who were so powerfully part . . . with the great dream, that now we had to admit that the great dream has faded and the truth is something else—that we'll never be any use. [Pp. 50–51]

Indeed, Anna's American lover's charge that she has been trying to "cage the truth" (p. 563) is itself made near the end of Anna's series of notebooks and counseling sessions, and Anna, after the change is made, admits that "it's no good."

Anna's fictional alter ego, Ella, reflects, quite naturally, the same attitudes as her creator. We are told, for instance, of Ella's awareness that a free woman, having "positively disdained ordinary morality," is not acceptable to the majority of either sex (p. 150). Ella's lover, Paul, tells her that the real revolution of the day is that of women against men (p. 184). Ella herself realizes that her emotions are "fitted for a kind of society that no longer exists," a monogamous society, and that she ought to have been a man (p. 269). Even more self-consciously than Anna, Ella prides herself on her independence, and is repeatedly reminded of this by her lovers. Ella comments to her friend, Julia, that "we've chosen to be free women, and this [i.e., sexual double standards and male indifference] is the price we pay" (p. 392). Julia's reply indicates the desperation both women feel: "Free! What's the use of us being free if they aren't? I swear to God, that every one of them, even the best of them, have the old idea of good women and bad women" (p. 392). The price paid, though, does not only include frustration and doubt, for Ella realizes that by being a "free woman," she has an advantage over wives, simply because she "was so much more exciting than the dull tied women" (p. 388). But, like Anna herself, who ultimately realizes that she is not free (p. 237), Ella must accept responsibility to be either free or happy. Anna wishes she were married, for instance, saying that she doesn't like living the way she does (p. 237), and Ella herself, we are told, "after years of freedom, is over-ready for a serious love" (p. 394).

Parenthetically, it should be mentioned that neither Anna nor Ella, in their self-conscious celebration of being "free women," approximates Mrs. Lessing's own attitude toward such freedom. She has said that she doesn't see herself as a "free woman" "only because I don't think anyone is 'free.'" [21] She also observed that "to imagine free man . . . is to step outside of what we are," for

> There is no one on this earth who is not twisted by fear and insecurity, and the compromises of thinking made inevitable by want and fear. . . . Slaves can envy the free; slaves can fight to free their children; but slaves suddenly set free are marked by the habits of submission; and slaves imagining freedom see it through the eyes of slaves. [22]

Hence this imagined freedom of Anna's and Ella's, as this chapter suggests, is not so much a total lack of individual responsibility as a series of gradually more intense and personal commitments, culminating, as the next part of this chapter will indicate, in the commitment to writing. Prior to that, though, we must consider the exact ways in which Anna's "emancipation" is expressed, through sexual attitudes and behavior, and through an obsessive self-understanding gained through psychoanalysis.

Throughout her life as recounted in the notebooks, and in her past youth as occasionally recalled in moments of stress or reminiscence, Anna thinks of herself in sexual terms, ranging from the trancelike "sexual obsession" felt at age fifteen (and which she would not go through again for an immense amount of money; pp. 88–89), to her subsequent simultaneous fear of and appeal for sexual experience, when she is first aware of her "emancipated" state (pp. 114–15), to the steps leading up to her defloration: petting (p. 118) and the initial act of sexual intercourse (referred to on p. 66). In each of the several "lives" she experiences, she has lovers who more or less correspond in their meaning for her with the gradually changing sense of commitment she acknowledges. In colonial Africa, for instance, it is Willi (with whom Anna is sexually incompatible; pp. 66–67), a relationship that ends when Willi discovers that Anna has just had intercourse with another man and, full of hatred, forces her into one last act of intercourse (p. 133). Later, involved with Michael, Anna moves into a more self-assured, yet still somewhat guilty, sexual relationship. The relationship itself seems based more on sex than on love (p. 289), but does not last long. Then Anna meets the American Communist, Nelson, who has a "moral fear of sex," and who "could never stay inside a woman for longer than a few seconds" (p. 413). A friend of Molly's from Ceylon, DeSilva, further complicates Anna's wishes for a satisfactory sexual experience, for he, first, picks up a strange girl on the street with whom he wants only sex, no feelings, and, later, sleeps with Anna, who justifies the act on the grounds that "it didn't matter to me" (p. 428). This too ends, for DeSilva wishes to use one of Anna's rooms for sex with another woman, so that Anna could hear the couple in bed (p. 429). Meeting an unnamed friend of Nelson's, Anna thinks, "A normal man at last, thank God" (p. 465), but this relationship ends because of the lack of warmth the man felt and because of his fear of his wife back home. All the men in this promiscuous sequence, quite clearly, are desperate choices for a love-partner for Anna, so it is small wonder that all the affairs end in a futile and sterile way.

But when Anna meets Saul Green, the American writer who aids in Anna's ultimate self-knowledge, she finds an entirely different sexual experience, even though there are the inevitable conflicts and arguments that affect their sexual rapport. Saul comes to Anna's apartment to rent a room, and upon their first meeting, gives Anna a close sexual examination (p. 470). Their mutual attraction is shown in Anna's similar examination of Saul:

> I saw his pose, standing with his back to the window in a way that was like a caricature of that young American we see in the films—sexy he-man, all balls and strenuous erection. He stood lounging, his thumbs hitched through his belt, fingers loose, but pointing as it were to his genitals. [P. 473]

Green subsequently refers to a "friend" (evidently himself) and the friend's sexual problems, and in the process he and Anna discuss the language inevitably used in discussing sex, with Anna accusing Saul of having an unhealthy attitude toward sex and Saul retorting by stating that he doesn't agree with the typically masculine double standard; later the same day, they have their first act of sexual intercourse (pp. 478–80). Anna senses that sex for Saul is a combination of emotions, as it is for her: she sees him as making love out of fear (of being alone, p. 481), out of hatred (a hard, violent sex, p. 491; cf. pp. 500, 524), and out of an indifference toward Anna's feelings (after he has just returned from making love with another woman, p. 486). Anna realizes that Saul's lovemaking is not a sadistic act (p. 494), but that he does appear to be loving someone else while in the act (pp. 497, 515). But sex with Saul is warm and fulfilling, as it has not been with the other men in Anna's life, and, important for Anna's psychological well-being, occurs spontaneously and quickly (p. 539).

Anna's other self, Ella, goes through somewhat the same sequence of lovers and emotions prior to her achieving a fulfilling sexual experience. But since Ella is a fictional creation of Anna's, Anna can put into Ella's consciousness and words many of the secret thoughts and socially embarrassing ideas about sex that Anna does not mention. After her first act of intercourse with a lover, Paul, Ella critically examines him and finds the experience "beautiful" (p. 168), at least in part because he was the first lover she had had in two years (p. 170). They again make love, gradually more mechanically and less beautifully (p. 174), even though she still senses the "instinctive warmth" (p. 176) radiated by Paul. But Ella cannot accept statements made by Paul that make her unhappy, so she mentally rejects his statement, "Odd isn't it, it really is true that if you love a woman sleeping with another woman means nothing" (p. 177). Later, briefly separated from Paul, she casually spends time with Cy Maitland, an American businessman. She is immediately attracted to Maitland, but for reasons she cannot wholly analyze. His behavior in bed, though, is completely self-centered and unconcerned for her feelings. Rapidly reaching orgasm, he repeatedly exclaims "Boy, Oh boy!" and talks of his wife. His attitude is suggested by his statements to Ella: "That's what I like. No problems with you" (p. 277), and "That's what I like about you—let's go to bed, you say, and that's fine and easy. I like you" (p. 278). After the ending of this unsatisfactory affair, Ella realizes that there is no point in her going to bed with anyone but Paul (p. 283). Later, Ella has intercourse with Jack, the efficient type of man who "has learned love-making out of a book. . . . [He] gets his pleasure from having got a woman into bed, not from sex itself" (pp. 388–89). Ella's next step, the nadir of her erotic career, comes when feelings of despair hit her:

> Now something new happens. She begins to suffer torments of sexual desire. Ella is frightened because she cannot remember feeling sexual desire, as a thing in it-

self, without reference to a specific man before, or at least not since her adolescence, and then it was always in relation to a fantasy about a man. Now she cannot sleep, she masturbates, to accompaniment of fantasies of hatred about men. Paul has vanished completely: she has lost the warm strong man of her experience, and can only remember a cynical betrayer. She suffers sex desire in a vacuum. She is acutely humiliated, thinking that this means she is dependent on men for "having sex," for "being serviced," for "being satisfied." She uses this kind of savage phrase to humiliate herself.

Then she realizes she is falling into a lie about herself, and about women, and that she must hold on to this knowledge: that when she was with Paul she felt no sex hungers that were not prompted by him; that if he was apart from her for a few days, she was dormant until he returned; that her present raging sexual hunger was not for sex, but was fed by all the emotional hungers of her life. That when she loved a man again, she would return to normal: a woman, that is, whose sexuality would ebb and flow in response to his. A woman's sexuality is, so to speak, contained by a man, if he is a real man; she is, in a sense, put to sleep by him, she does not think about sex. [P. 390]

But despite these thoughts, she again succumbs to the temptation of a brief affair, this time with a Canadian scriptwriter; she again "feels nothing," and believes that the act was "something he set himself to do and that's all" (p. 391), i.e., an act of accomplishment, not an act of feeling.

In these furtive acts of intercourse, Ella, like Anna, discovers that although she can give pleasure, she does not receive it herself unless she has a deep emotional commitment to the man; indeed, Ella reflects, when she is with the Canadian writer, that she "has not had a real orgasm since Paul left her" (p. 391), and with Maitland, she realizes that it is even more complicated:

Ella was thinking: But with Paul, I would have come in that time—so what's wrong?—it's not enough to say, I don't love this man? She understood suddenly that she would never come with this man. She thought: for women like me, integrity isn't chastity, it isn't fidelity, it isn't any of the old words. Integrity is the orgasm. That is something I haven't any control over. I could never have an orgasm with this man, I can give pleasure and that's all. But why not? Am I saying that I can never come except with a man I love? Because what sort of a desert am I condemning myself to if that's true? [Pp. 278–79]

As an indication that the matter of orgasm is extremely central to the sexual commitment made by both Anna and Ella, Mrs. Lessing provides one lengthy passage in which both Anna and Ella occur. Anna mentions at first that the "difficulty of writing about sex, for women, is that sex is best when not thought about, not analyzed. Women deliberately choose not to think about technical sex. They get irritable when men talk technically, it's out of self-preservation: they want to preserve the spontaneous emotion that is essential for their satisfaction" (p. 185). After reflecting about a broken marriage, caused, as she was told, by the husband's too-small penis, Anna begins describing Ella's and her own sexual experiences in as clinical a tone as elsewhere in the book is condemned by Anna:

When Ella first made love with Paul, during the first few months, what set the seal on the fact she loved him, and made it possible for her to use the word, was that she immediately experienced orgasm. Vaginal orgasm that is. And she could not have experienced it if she had not loved him. It is the orgasm that is created by the man's need for a woman, and his confidence in that need.

As time went on, he began to use mechanical means. (I look at the word mechanical—a man wouldn't use it.) Paul began to rely on manipulating her externally, on giving Ella clitoral orgasms. Very exciting. Yet there was always a part of her that resented it. Because she felt that the fact he wanted to, was an expression of his in-

stinctive desire not to commit himself to her. She felt
that without knowing it or being conscious of it . . .
he was afraid of the emotion. The vaginal orgasm is emotion and nothing else, felt as emotion and expressed in
sensations that are indistinguishable from emotion. The
vaginal orgasm is a dissolving in a vague, dark generalised
sensation like being swirled in a warm whirlpool. There
are several different sorts of clitoral orgasms, and they
are more powerful (that is a male word) than the vaginal orgasm. There can be a thousand thrills, sensations,
etc., but there is only one real female orgasm and that is
when a man, from the whole of his need and desire takes
a woman and wants all her response. Everything else is
a substitute and a fake, and the most inexperienced
woman feels this instinctively. Ella had never experienced clitoral orgasm before Paul, and she told him so,
and he was delighted. . . . But when she told him she
had never experienced what she insisted on calling "a
real orgasm" to anything like the same depth before him,
he involuntarily frowned. . . . As time went on, the emphasis shifted in their love-making from the real orgasm
to the clitoral orgasm, and there came a point when Ella
realized . . . that she was no longer having real orgasms.
That was before the end, when Paul left her. In short,
she knew emotionally what the truth was when her mind
would not admit it. [Pp. 186–87]

Just prior to the end of their time together, Paul leaves the
country and Ella is thereafter incapable, as already mentioned, of achieving orgasm with any other lover. As she
says later,

And what about us? Free, we say, yet the truth is that
they get erections when they're with a woman they don't
give a damn about, but we don't get an orgasm unless we
love him. What's free about that? [P. 392]

The "new mood or phase" in which Ella finds herself, she
says, "is only the opposite side of being possessed by sex";

she now says she "cannot believe she will ever feel desire again" (p. 393).

The "Free Women" sections of *The Golden Notebook*, finally, suggests even more of Anna's deep concern with the inadequacies of a sexual commitment. Marion, Anna's friend in these sections of the book, tells Anna that she hates going to bed, even though it was once the "happiest time" of her life, when she was still a newlywed. She indicates that Richard, her lover, has to "make himself" have intercourse with her, and asks Anna if she had ever slept with a man when she knew he was forcing himself to do so (p. 238). Both Anna and Marion are concerned with what they call a "real man" (instead of the "little boys and homosexuals and half-homosexuals" in England; p. 245), and Anna goes so far as to wish for such a man for her daughter's sake (p. 334), evidently as a proxy father. Later Anna says to Milton, the American writer, that she has had her fill of "cold and efficient sex," after which he asks, "what's happened to all that warm and committed sex we read about in books?" He also says that "love is too difficult," to which Anna retorts, "And sex too cold" (pp. 560–61). As if to support this statement by Anna, Milton shortly thereafter abruptly asks her, "Want me to screw you?" (p. 564). Anna replies that "there's something about a man with a whacking great erection that it's hard to resist" (p. 565), but they nonetheless separate, for Anna has made the discovery that "committed sex," as Milton calls it, is too insubstantial and dissatisfying a commitment for either her emotional security or her sense of identity.

It is, in fact, her search for her identity that leads Anna to go to and depend upon a lay psychoanalyst [23] named Mrs. Marks, but who Anna usually refers to as "Mother Sugar." Anna recounts various dreams she has had to Mother Sugar, most of which are nightmares—of sheer terror (pp. 408–9), of sexual attack and sex-reversal (pp. 481, 516), of the mad Charlie Themba (pp. 506–7), of a film projectionist showing her own life (pp. 422, 525–29, 541–43), and of her own death (p. 512). The terrible dreams themselves parallel the emotional moods Anna ex-

periences in her waking hours, and one dream in particular
(in addition to the apocalyptic dream mentioned earlier of
the Communist world) warrants fuller treatment:

> I dreamed I held a kind of casket in my hands, and in-
> side it was something very precious. . . . There was a
> small crowd of people . . . waiting for me to hand them
> the casket. I was incredibly happy that at last I could
> give them this precious object. But when I handed it
> over, I saw suddenly they were all business men, brokers,
> something like that. They did not open the box, but
> started handing me large sums of money. I began to cry.
> I shouted: "open the box, open the box," but they
> couldn't hear me, or wouldn't listen. Suddenly I saw
> they were all characters in some film or play, and that I
> had written it, and was ashamed of it. . . . I was a char-
> acter in my own play. I opened the box and forced them
> to look. But instead of a beautiful thing, which I thought
> would be there, there was a mass of fragments, but bits
> and pieces from everywhere, all over the world—I recog-
> nized a lump of red earth, that I knew came from Africa,
> and then a bit of metal that came off a gun from Indo-
> China, and then everything was horrible, bits of flesh
> from people killed in the Korean War and a communist
> party badge off someone who died in a Soviet prison.
> This, looking at the mass of ugly fragments, was so pain-
> ful that I couldn't look, and I shut the box. But the
> group of businessmen or money-people hadn't noticed.
> They took the box from me and opened it. I turned
> away so not to see, but they were delighted. At last I
> looked and I saw that there was something in the box.
> It was a small green crocodile with a winking sardonic
> snout. I thought it was the image of a crocodile, made of
> jade, or emeralds, then I saw it was alive, for large frozen
> tears rolled down its cheeks and turned into diamonds.
> I laughed out loud when I saw how I had cheated the
> businessmen and I woke up. [Pp. 215–16]

While a precise and full analysis of this dream is clearly
impossible, there are several points that must be made. In
the first place, this dream of Anna's parallels her own life

in several points. Some of the men with whom Anna (and Ella) have had affairs have been businessmen, and these have uniformly been unresponsive to feminine needs; they have, in a word, treated that which is beautiful and prized as a mercenary thing. Anna's own fragmented life is also suggested by this dream. And the crocodile is suggested by the letter from Charlie Themba, referred to above, in which he insanely envisions a crocodile devouring him. Thus this dream contains in capsule, symbolic form the several elements of Anna's own life, focused as they are in terms of a film or scenario with Anna as the author. Evidently death is the outcome of all the various earlier struggles—racial, political, sexual—that Anna has experienced, if, that is, she is able to "cheat" the "businessman." And this is, I believe, suggested by Anna's final dream, described in the last "Free Women" section of the novel:

> One afternoon she went to sleep and dreamed. She knew it was a dream she had often had before, in one form or another. She had two children. One was Janet, plump and glossy with health. The other was Tommy, a small baby, and she was starving him. Her breasts were empty, because Janet had had all the milk in them; and so Tommy was thin and puny, dwindling before her eyes from starvation. He vanished altogether, in a tiny coil of pale bony starving flesh, before she woke, which she did in a fever of anxiety, self-division and guilt. Yet, awake, she could see no reason why she should have dreamed of Tommy being starved by her. And besides, she knew that in other dreams of this cycle, the "starved" figure might be anyone, perhaps someone she passed in the street whose face had haunted her. Yet there was no doubt she felt responsible for this half-glimpsed person, for why otherwise should she dream of having failed him—or her?
>
> After this dream, she went feverishly back to work, cutting out news items, fastening them to the wall. [Pp. 556–57]

This dream appears to suggest that Anna's fragmented self has extended to her two children in the dream, with the "starved" one being any person with whom she comes in contact. Her sense of responsibility is focused on this "starved" person, whoever it might be at the moment, but responsibility, at this point, can only take the cathartic form of the frantic newspaper clipping and pasting discussed in the last section of this chapter; it is, in brief, a preliminary step in Anna's ultimate self-knowledge and acceptance of both herself and the world around her. It is significant, also, to note that there is one child in this dream that is "plump and glossy with health"; the obsessive terror and wasteland effects of most of her other dreams are ameliorated slightly by this image of fertility and plenty.

Mother Sugar's counseling of Anna is thus the specific means by which Anna is gradually able to see herself in perspective and to gain control of her own life. One lengthy exchange between the two women (pp. 402–5) is central to any complete understanding of the forces that effect such a change in Anna, and is especially concerned with Anna's leaving the relative safety of her dreams and the world of "myth" they contain, and going forth on her own. No matter how horrible the dreams, Anna says, "all the pain, and the killing and the violence are safely held in the story and . . . can't hurt me" (p. 402). Anna sees that "the individual recognizes one part after another of his earlier life as an aspect of the general human experience" (p. 403), and (further supporting the obvious Jungian emphasis) that

> What I did then, what I felt then, is only the reflection of that great archetypal dream, or epic story, or stage in history, then he is free, because he has separated himself from the experience, or fitted it like a mosaic into a very old pattern, and by the act of setting it into place, is free of the individual pain of it. [P. 403]

After Anna says that she is "living the kind of life women never lived before" (p. 403), Mother Sugar asks,

> In what way are you different? Are you saying there haven't been artist-women before? There haven't been women who were independent? There haven't been women who insisted on sexual freedom? I tell you, there

are a great line of women stretching out behind you into the past, and you have to seek them out and find them in yourself and be conscious of them. [P. 404]

After raising several objections, Anna says that she wants "to separate in herself what is old and cyclic, the recurring history, the myth, from what is new, what I feel or think that might be new. . . . Sometimes I meet people, and it seems to me the fact they are cracked across, they're split, means they are keeping themselves open for something" (pp. 404–5). Mother Sugar's technique, quite clearly, is to ask Anna probing questions which force her to see herself in perspective and to see what she really is in the deepest recesses of her psyche. She does not leave Anna in the fragmented chaotic past, but instead, by the "shock of recognition," forces her to see the present and future as they really are, potentially coherent and ordered and fruitful.

Anna, though, cannot receive this ordered existence vicariously from Mother Sugar; she must work it out for and by herself, and this is done through her obsessive concern with language and with putting on paper the ordered language constituting human discourse. Paralleling her sessions and conversations with Mother Sugar are Anna's frantic efforts to record, in fragmented form, all the experiences of her several disparate "selves," in the notebooks that constitute the bulk of *The Golden Notebook*, and gradually to go beyond the limitations of private communication to express to others, through a novel, her affirmation of ongoing life and structured personal existence.

As Mrs. Lessing says in her personal credo, "The Small Personal Voice," commitment to writing is necessary because of today's confusion of standards and values; because of the compassion, warmth, humanity, and love of people to be found in the truly great novels; because the writer has a responsibility as a human being to choose for evil or to strengthen good; and—most important of all—because the writer's recognition of man as an individual is necessary if the novel as a genre is to regain greatness. To achieve greatness, Mrs. Lessing states that the novelist's "small, personal voice" must re-create "warmth and humanity and love of people," [24] especially if a "great age of literature" like the nineteenth century is to result. Such a credo does not, Mrs. Lessing believes, necessarily become "propagandizing" for a cause, political or otherwise; nor does the novelist necessarily regress by so committing himself. Rather, the novelist "must feel himself as an instrument of change for good or bad," as an "architect of the soul." [25] Not only can such ideas be said to apply to Mrs. Lessing herself, they also apply quite well to her protagonist in *The Golden Notebook*, Anna Freeman Wulf.

As *The Golden Notebook* opens, Anna Wulf is living as a divorcée in London, supporting herself and her daughter by the residual royalties from a successful novel, *Frontiers of War*, which is in turn based on Anna's earlier life in colonial Africa. As Anna attempts to make sense of her life, she puts down in four notebooks—black, red, yellow, and blue—her memories and feelings. In the black notebook, Anna writes her own account of her time in Central Africa during World War II, and the events leading up to the writing of *Frontiers of War*. Anna's feelings concerning this book are equivocal: she simultaneously depends upon the book's earnings, and knows it to be a failure (pp. 59–60). And later, when the many financial solicitations for her novel by film companies pour in, Anna's feeling of revulsion against the world of communism is made all the more pronounced (p. 243). She ultimately does sell the film rights—three times, in fact—but never with any conviction that the book would be filmed (p. 464); and on one occasion she refuses a studio's offer when the representative arrives (pp. 471–72). And, finally, when Anna does again write (the autobiographical novel called *Free Women*), she conceives of herself as being glad when one of her lovers said he did not like *Frontiers of War* (p. 562).

As already mentioned, Anna's black notebook deals with her life in Africa and the red her life as a Communist. The yellow notebook, by contrast, is Anna's novelistic attempt to see herself in perspective, by means of a thinly disguised fictional alter ego, Ella, whose circumstances and personal life are quite like Anna's. Anna had mentioned earlier, in discussing the Communist party, that the ogre of capitalism—from a Communist viewpoint—could be "supplanted by others, like communist, or woman's magazine" (p. 296). It is no surprise, then, that Ella works for a woman's magazine, nor that she had written part of a novel (p. 149). This fictional work in which Ella appears is entitled *The Shadow of the Third*, a reference, as Anna later explained it, to "the woman altogether better than I was" (p. 545). But this woman does not remain static; she is at first the wife of Paul, Ella's lover; then she becomes "Ella's younger *alter ego* formed from fantasies about Paul's wife," and she finally becomes Ella herself (pp. 384–85). The bulk of the yellow notebook, however, concerns Ella's gradual completion of her novel (it is barely half-finished as the notebook begins; p. 151). The initial idea, she says, came "when she found herself getting dressed to go out to dine with people after she had told herself she did not want to go out" (p. 152). The difficulty she has with the writing, though, is not technical; we are told that "it was as if the story were already written somewhere inside herself" (p. 152). Just as Ella is Anna's alter ego, so Ella conceives of her novel as a reflection of herself, as "carrying on conversations with one's image in the looking-glass" (p. 153). Similarly, just as Anna can "read" Ella's story, so Ella sees her own novel as being already written and with herself reading it (p. 182). Ella's novel is accepted for publication, and Ella sees it as having the same basic quality that Anna had earlier wished the Communist novels would have: honesty (p. 184). For, as Anna herself says later concerning the yellow notebook,

> It frightens me that when I'm writing I seem to have some awful second sight, or something like it, an intuition of some kind; a kind of intelligence is at work that is much too painful to use in ordinary life; one couldn't live at all if one used it for living. [P. 489]

And just as those in Anna's Communist period who had experienced the most loneliness frequently turned to writing for meaning in an otherwise meaningless existence, so Ella too discovers that, for herself as well as for others, writing is a kind of therapy. Ella discovers, for instance, that her father, "alone, withdrawing from his wife into books and the dry, spare dreams of a man who might have been a poet or a mystic" (p. 398), is in fact both; but, significantly, his poems are about "solitude, loss, fortitude, the adventures of isolation" (p. 398).

For Ella, though, this isolation continues beyond the vicarious act of writing out, as a form of therapy, her emotions and sense of isolation. After the conversation with her father, she looks "for the outlines of a story" and finds, "again and again, nothing but patterns of defeat, death, irony." She refuses these; she fails to force "patterns of happiness of simple life"; but she finally finds it possible to "accept the patterns of self-knowledge which mean unhappiness or at least a dryness," and which could be twisted into a victory. That is, by searching in the negative "patterns," she can, she hopes, twist a positive "pattern" into shape. And by conceiving of a man and a woman, "both at the end of their tether," "both cracking up because of a deliberate attempt to transcend their own limits," a "new kind of strength" is found. She waits, we are told, "for the images to form, to take on life" (pp. 399–400). But instead of "life," we are given a series of nineteen synopses of short stories or short novels, all of which are counterparts or summaries of events in the four notebooks or in the "Free Women" sections of The Golden Notebook, and all of which are expanded in the final portion of the yellow notebook, in the comments Anna makes (Ella has now been completely dropped from the narrative) about her relationship with Saul Green, an American. Saul is quite like Anna in his sense of defeatedness and spiritual and emotional isolation, and closely approximates Paul, in the earlier portions of the yellow notebook. He is particularly and acutely aware of Anna's attempt to make notations in a series of fragmented diaries (the four notebooks) a substitute for a direct encounter with her problems, with life, with her need to write. He asks, on one occasion, "Instead of making a record of my sins in your diary, why don't you write another novel?" (p. 516). Anna's retort that she has a "writer's block," of course, neither deters nor persuades Green; his comment has sufficiently disturbed Anna that she decides to begin a fifth notebook (the golden one mentioned in the novel's title), which Saul requests of her.

Instead of giving away the new notebook, Anna decides to pack away the other four notebooks and to start the new one—"all of myself in one book" (p. 519). In this golden notebook, the relationship between Anna and Green continues and is finally broken off, but with each providing the first sentence for a novel by the other; Green's finished novel, we are told, "was later published and did rather well" (p. 550). But Anna's initial sentence serves as the beginning of the *Free Women* novel which, like the four major notebooks, is divided into parts; the fifth and last of these parts concludes *The Golden Notebook*, and is her primary method of using writing as a therapeutic measure.

The blue notebook, about which little has been said thus far, is primarily a factual diary-account of Anna's experiences in analysis and of her near-madness and is designed to be a contrast to the "fictional" qualities found in the other notebooks. Anna Wulf is forced in this notebook to face her nearly overwhelming fear of war and "of the real movement of the world towards dark, hardening power" (p. 503), and as a result provides the novel's most searing criticism of society. The diary entries run from 1950 to 1956 without major omissions, but the eighteen months from March 1956 to September 1957 are described without dates and concern Anna's initial experiences with Saul Green.

The "Free Women" portions of *The Golden Notebook* are in some respects more enlightening than anything else in the book, and are certainly to be considered an integral part of the major narrative of the novel, since the events described in these portions (occurring in 1957) are chronologically the closest to the present. Evidently ironically, Mrs. Lessing has said, "The structure of the whole book says that this little novel (i.e., "Free Women") came out of all that mass of experience." [26] But since the point of *The Golden Notebook* is, as Mrs. Lessing has said elsewhere,[27] "the relation of its parts to each other," the "Free Women" sections must be considered as relevant, even if ironically so, as the notebooks themselves.

The first four (of five) parts entitled "Free Women" closely match what is known of Anna from the notebooks, with the difference, as was mentioned above, primarily one of chronnology. These portions of the book deal particularly with a friend of Anna's, Molly Jacobs, and her son, Tommy, who is closest to Anna in the sense that he knows her better than anyone else. Molly's former husband (and Tommy's father), Richard, knows Anna well enough to allude to her "complicated ideas about writing" (p. 38), and he also points out that she is afraid of writing what she really thinks about life, since this would make her expose herself emotionally and thus lead to isolation (p. 39). Anna says to Molly that her notebooks are "chaos" (p. 41), but to Tommy Anna admits much more. To his question about her four notebooks ("Why not one notebook?" p. 226), Anna replies, "Perhaps because it would be such a— scramble. Such a mess." And Tommy, aware of the pressures at work in Anna's mind (evident primarily because of similar pressures which lead to his own futile suicide attempt later), asks the question no one can state without self-incrimination: "Why shouldn't it be a mess?" (p. 226). Tommy also examines Anna's four notebooks, an act no one but Saul Green otherwise is described as doing. Anna explains her notebook habit by saying that she keeps "trying to write the truth and realising it's not true" (p. 233), to which Tommy retorts, "Perhaps it is true; perhaps it is, and you can't bear it, so you cross it out" (p. 233). Later, in an exhausted, near-delirious state, Anna sees herself,

> seated on the music-stool, writing, writing; making an entry in one book, then ruling it off, or crossing it out; she saw the pages patterned with different kinds of writing; divided, bracketed, broken—she felt a swaying nausea; and then saw Tommy, not herself, standing with his

> lips pursed in concentration, turning the pages of her
> orderly notebooks. [P. 332]

The ironic word "orderly" is of course unintentional because of Anna's mental condition at the time it was uttered,
for if any one point is made repeatedly, it is that Anna's
diaries (unlike Saul Green's, for example, which run chronologically; p. 448) are chaotic, like her life. And when Saul
later asks her the same question Tommy had asked earlier,
about her four notebooks, she replies (putting away three
of the four while speaking), "Obviously, because it's been
necessary to split myself up, but from now on I shall be
using one only" (p. 511). Anna had neglected her notebooks after Tommy's attempted suicide, and had wondered
if his attempt had been "triggered off by reading her notebooks" (p. 566). But Anna herself has been reading Saul's
diaries, until the moment when she knows she will never
again do so (pp. 540–41; but see also p. 460), primarily because she has been able to manipulate the tangled lives of
two isolated people, herself and Saul, and to find some
meaning in life itself.

It is in Anna's frenzied efforts to find meaning in life that
the most chaotic expressions of her obsession with writing
and with words are to be found. Shortly after she was first
advised to keep a diary, in 1950 (p. 205), Anna began the
practice of cutting out and pasting—in the notebooks or on
the walls of her room—carefully dated newspaper clippings.
Seven years later, toward the novel's conclusion, Anna is
still, and perhaps even more so, concerned with such clippings (pp. 555–56). Anna once again turns to her notebooks, neglected since Tommy's accident, but she feels
alien to them, so, faster than ever, she cuts out newspaper
clippings. Even though Anna, in these frenzied activities,
approaches a psychotic state, she has always had the same
obsession with masses of newspapers and magazines. But all
these hysterical episodes with newspapers are but a prelude
to the ultimate experience, which occurs toward the book's
end.

After having missed the newspapers for a week (significantly, the things Anna realizes she has missed are "a war here, a dispute there"; p. 502), Anna moves "forward into a new knowledge, a new understanding" based on her fear (p. 503). In brief, this entire newspaper obsession serves as contrast or perhaps counterpoint to the major concern Anna senses with regard to her sanity, namely, the use and effects of written words. And while Anna's ultimate "cure" (if such is the word) for her malaise is her writing the novel entitled *Free Women*, such of the mental calm she achieves obviously comes through the medium of newspapers. For after she satisfactorily resolves her feverish obsession with newspapers, Anna looks at the blue notebook, in which these events are recorded, and thinks, "if I could write in it Anna would come back, but I could not make my hand go out to take up the pen" (p. 511). But after she discovers who she is, with the help of Saul Green, who is also lost and isolated, she is able to write again, with the result being, of course, the "Free Women" passages. Previously, Anna had turned "everything into fiction," which she then concluded was "an evasion" (p. 197). She also asks herself why she can not put down, simply, the real events in her life and in others' lives, with the answer that such fictionizing is "simply a means of concealing something" from herself (p. 197). But after her return from the world of insanity and chaos, she finally does become capable of stating, through the medium of fiction, her true feelings and experiences.

The self-knowledge which seems to be at the heart of Mrs. Lessing's theme in *The Golden Notebook* is clearly, then, necessary for mental equilibrium and emotional stability, and is, at least in the case of Anna Wulf, capable of being gained through a psychological and mental descent into hell. But the written and printed word is especially important for Anna; hence the ultimate resolution of her particular mental and emotional problems is necessarily bound up in and with and through writing. Through writing—public writing, such as a novel, not private writing, such as the notebooks—Anna is able to relate meaningfully again to the world and to those she knows. Just as the earlier commitments Anna had made have proven false or insufficient or inadequate, so her final commitment proves true and sufficient and adequate. Although others can be committed to other causes, writers like Anna must, in Mrs. Lessing's words, re-create "warmth and humanity and love of people" in their writing. No longer can Anna remain neutral, uninvolved in the lives of others (as she certainly is in much of this book, particularly in the case of her passivity and unconcern at Tommy's attempted suicide), or unattached. She must become, again in Mrs. Lessing's terms, an "instrument of change for good or bad," an "architect of the soul." And since Anna, primarily through her commitment to writing, does find it possible to become these things, one can say with little hesitation, because of the personal struggle in which the protagonist is involved and the satisfactory victory that protagonist gains over her weaker self, that *The Golden Notebook* is very much in the line of the memorable nineteenth-century novels Mrs. Lessing cites as being the "highest point of literature" [28]—those by Tolstoy, Stendhal, Dostoevsky, Balzac, Turgenev, and Chekhov.

Anna Wulf, then, is herself no more "free" than those she knew in the Communist party or in Africa or in any of several other earlier commitments; indeed, her very name suggests this symbolically, for she has ceased to be a "Free/man" when she married; then she became a "Wulf," not unlike the wolves of destruction she had earlier envisioned in her nightmares. But if absolute "freedom" is not possible in this world, then commitment is, and on this point Mrs. Lessing has been most explicit:

> The act of getting a story or novel published is an act of communication, an attempt to impose one's personality and beliefs on other people. If a writer accepts this responsibility, he must see himself . . . as an architect of the soul.[29]

And in so communicating, Anna is paradoxically exercising the very quality mentioned above as impossible in our world, the freedom of the individual—the freedom to fight, to "push boulders," to write for others, to work responsibly to improve the world, to try to eliminate personal and social chaos, to see ourselves as we really are. The "commitment to freedom," then, is both relative and continually in need of reexamination and modification as life goes on. Even if such "freedom" is never attained, it is the goal which keeps us sane and able to handle the many pressures of human life responsibly. Mrs. Lessing has referred to a "resting-point, a place of decision, hard to reach and precariously balanced." She goes on to say:

> It is a balance which must be continually tested and reaffirmed. Living in the midst of this whirlwind of change, it is impossible to make final judgements or absolute statements of value. The point of rest should be the writer's recognition of man, the responsive individual, voluntarily submitting his will to the collective, but never finally; and insisting on making his own personal and private judgements before every act of submission.[30]

Certainly Mrs. Lessing, in and through such profound and rich works as *The Golden Notebook*, has made this "recognition of man, the responsive individual." This is no small task for any writer, and Mrs. Lessing has generally succeeded in demonstrating in her longer fiction the extent to which she has mastered it. To be sure, there are points on which Mrs. Lessing can be criticized, as in her handling of character and situation, but these are, I believe, of less significance than her accomplishment in detailing the experiences and development of such highly sensitive, intelligent, and self-analytic women as Anna Wulf.

5

Retreat to Innocence and
Briefing for a Descent into Hell

Doris Lessing has published two additional novels, one a minor work she has repeatedly—and correctly—noted as an inferior piece of work, and another more recent one somewhat outside the range of this study. The first, *Retreat to Innocence*, her fourth novel, was published in 1956, shortly after Mrs. Lessing had left England for a seven-weeks' trip home to Southern Rhodesia; the second, *Briefing for a Descent into Hell*, was published early in 1971.

Retreat to Innocence[1] concerns a two-dimensional heroine, Julia Barr, naïve and virginal daughter of a prominent Briton, Sir Andrew Barr, who becomes initiated sexually and politically by a Czech refugee, Jan Brod, an active Communist. Julia's expectations for life are conventionally bourgeois, and at the book's end, when Jan and his brother Franz return to the Continent, Julia initiates a young man named Roger sexually and in time marries him for the comforts she really desires in life. As in Mrs. Lessing's other books, the conflict of generations is especially well drawn, not merely in moral terms but even more in the differing attitudes toward political activism and commitment. Though Julia rejects romantic love as a criterion for male-female relations, Jan, ironically, holds "personal relations" to be more important than anything else in life. For Julia's problem, as with Anna Wulf, is that she is a divided person, and at the book's end she reflects on her lack of capacity of doing anything with an "undivided mind."

It is in Julia's sexual relationships, not surprisingly, where her own unconventionality and emancipation seem especially pertinent. After defloration by Jan, she reflects on such reactions as guilt, self-accusation, and so on. Yet despite her new-found liberation, she continues naïvely to be shocked at sex-talk until her marriage to Roger, at which time she finds sex to be as "simple as breathing." Hence the book's title, *Retreat to Innocence*, is ironic in that Julia, though no longer conventionally "pure" (white wedding gown to the contrary), does "retreat" to a safer, less ambiguous world of conventionality and stability than she has known with Jan.

Jan, an intellectual, demonstrates a subtle differentiation of behavior and attitude toward life and especially government that is radically alien both to Julia and to the various other Britons he encounters. He knows rationally, for example, what awaits him back in Czechoslovakia, and he is wholly opposed to bureaucracy, whether Communist or capitalist; yet he shows a dedication to communism far beyond anyone else in Mrs. Lessing's fiction. He knows rationally too that the party makes mistakes and that it changes, though he does differ from the fanatical true-believer he resembles in such other respects as in his awareness of the relationship of art to politics. With a breadth of knowledge about literature and culture in general, he sees the pernicious effects of censorship and sensationalism. Julia's awareness of the world situation is derived wholly from books, while Jan's is based on living and on writing his own accounts of life in peasant villages, and even a monstrous quarter-million-word allegory combining the story of Jesus and Communist theory. In every respect, then, Jan is involved and committed to the causes he espouses, while Julia distantly and objectively tries to avoid involvement. Hence Julia (and her entire generation, by extension) misses the very thing she says she believes in above all and wishes to maintain: her individuality and freedom, seen especially in her choosing the bland Roger for comfort and security. But Jan voluntarily gives up his freedom in the democratic world to return to the country of his youth; while Julia can only mouth the platitudes of uninvolvement, Jan has the privilege to choose and the ethical responsibility of following up such a decision in his life. Julia is not even free to follow Jan to the Continent, for this would constitute a denial of her bourgeois desires in life and her supposed, self-declared freedom from commitment. Jan, as a representative of the "reality principle" in life, contrasts with Julia, who cannot face reality directly for long; she prefers the safe, conventional world she has dreamed of for so long. In withdrawing from making any commitment, Julia has by that very refusal to act committed herself irrevocably to a far more anarchistic existence than that which she believes Jan has.

As mentioned earlier, the book is a minor work, and Mrs. Lessing's admissions of its inferiority [2] constitute a refreshingly candid appraisal by an author of her work. Of course, as a polemic or apologia for a particular political theory one would not necessarily expect fully developed characters and consistently clear motivation, for the emphasis is not on writing a novel as such so much as on defending a particular thesis. Nonetheless, the book does develop a number of the themes and emphases found in her other, admittedly more mature, fiction, such as commitment and freedom. But the neat oversimplification of character and situation are more responsible for the book's minor status than any failure of conception, and even when commitment is lacking, as in Julia's case at the book's conclusion, we are aware of the emphasis on that trait. For when commitment is lacking, we find emptiness, sterility of desire, meaningless relationships, and a refusal to act in making personal decisions. Ironically, the book was published just prior to Mrs. Lessing's leaving the Communist party, an act itself demonstrating personal conviction of a high order. And, further, although Anna Wulf in *The Golden Notebook* also hesitated to act, that book, as we have seen, is both as a novel and as a statement of dedicated commitment superior to *Retreat to Innocence*.

As coruscating a literary event as the publication of *The Four-Gated City* was in 1969, the publication of *Briefing for a Descent into Hell* in 1971 [3] was even more cause for acclaim. For this newest novel by Doris Lessing departs radically from anything else she has ever written in several major ways, although the same dominant themes of mental imbalance and psychic phenomena emphasized in *The Golden Notebook* and in the last of the Martha Quest novels are to be found here. For one change from the earlier books, the protagonist is male: Charles Watkins, a classics professor at Cambridge, whose mental odyssey and restoration to psychological health constitute the essence of the book. Mrs. Lessing calls this new work "inner-space fiction," an attempt to probe beneath the layers of social pretense and the façade of conventionality that so often is a substitute for a deeper reality. The book, furthermore, is experimental in a way none of the others (with the exception, again, of *The Golden Notebook*) happens to be: although the central narrative, the reader sees upon finishing the book, is a movement from "insanity" to "sanity" (the words themselves are misleading), Watkins believes he is doomed to circle the Atlantic on a raft endlessly, after a "Crystal," an extraterrestrial space vehicle, takes his companions but rejects him. In time he lands on a paradisiacal island on which he finds a ruined prehistoric city. Soon creatures combining the features of rats and dogs move into the deserted city, followed by apes; in time ferocious war breaks out between these two species, leading to utter carnage. Watkins is flown to safety by a gigantic white bird, which then returns him to the clearing where the Crystal again comes, this time claiming him and bringing him back to "reality."

At this point—roughly one-third the way through the book—Watkins is transported to a celestial gathering of Greek deities who debate ways of sending eternal beings down to Earth to become infants, a kind of Wordsworthian loss of innocence and divinity as human consciousness develops. At this point Watkins is found wandering aimlessly in London and is admitted to a mental ward in a hospital where the bulk of the book takes place. He cannot remember his earthly life as an academician at all, but can remember previous "existences" such as being a guerrilla fighter in Yugoslavia during World War II. After extended hospitalization and application of drugs, during which he remembers nothing at all of his family, previous life as a teacher, or close friends, he is given shock treatment and, in a disappointingly abrupt dénouement, is restored to "normality." Throughout, the implication is that Watkins's "dream" life or "fantasy" is far more real and memorable than the rather dull academic life he had lived; indeed, such "real" encroachments upon his consciousness as the two attending physicians are dismissed as "not there," though one of the two does in time break through the veneer of fantasy. Watkins, obviously, has gone through a mental breakdown, brought on by forces and pressures never specified; and were it not for the shock treatment—itself questioned in the novel as possibly an invalid intrusion into the privacy of one's mind—Watkins would have found his "fantasy" world both more appealing and more enduring than the flatness of everyday life.

The title itself refers to the conversation of Greek deities: Mercury reflects on the others' willingness to go "down" to Earth, a "Poisonous Hell," and of the impossibility of doing so and remaining unaffected by earthly life. Truth, Mercury says, will be "part of humanity's new soon-to-be-developed equipment," thanks not to such as he but rather to the celestial light who is equated with both God and with clarity of insight into the meaning of life. A further Wordsworthian suggestion is found in two isolated incidents in the book, adding to the matter of light/darkness, heaven/hell, etc., as contrasts. While in the deserted city, Watkins sees a rat-creature simultaneously giving birth to young, trying to defend herself (and her brood) from attack by other creatures (and incidentally killing some of her own young), and in finally giving birth to the doomed young as her crazed antagonist attempts to copulate with her—an awesome, grotesque combination of birth and death. Then, when with the Yugoslavian guerrillas, Watkins's beloved is killed by a doe defending a newly born fawn. Similarly, the descent into hell for which the celestial creatures are briefed is both a going into life through birth and an acquiescence into death, into mortality. Toward the end of his convalescence, Watkins comments that

"There are lots of things in our ordinary life that are—shadows. Like coincidences, or dreamings, the kind of thing that are an angle to ordinary life. . . . The important thing is this—to remember that some things reach out to us from that level of living, to here. Anxiety is one. The sense of urgency." When he was first exploring the jungle around the deserted city, he observed, "There is no way of making himself immune to the different person that may come to life in him at any moment—and who does not know the laws of being of his host. But I was already beginning to doubt that I knew who was stronger, which was host, what was myself and what a perverted offshoot." Hence the first glimpse of the dog-rat creature seems alien to Watkins in every way, and the apes similar to him; it is, in a word, as if man's darker nature were manifested in animal form.

The book's concern, then, is with the amorphous and vague demarcation between extremes of being. And this is suggested even further by Watkins's observation that the sea had been the "well of sanity" he had known prior to being washed ashore; similarly, "sanity" becomes subsequently whichever sphere of existence Watkins finds most "real," and thus his university status becomes "unreal." And time, so often a force to contend with in Mrs. Lessing's fiction, again becomes not a tangible part of the "real" but a relative, shadowy, unclear "shifting of gears," to use Watkins's term, between two or more disparate consciousnesses. Indeed, Watkins is able for a time to stand in perspective to his own circumstances and to see two identities become one. Hence wholeness becomes, again as in *The Golden Notebook*, the prime consideration in this novel; and when one senses that he has experienced an occurrence previously, the phenomenon known as *déjà vu* (and which has been found in Mrs. Lessing's earlier novels as well), he senses the ultimate similarity and identity existing among portions of various earthly entities or organisms. For man, despite the extremes to which he goes, is ultimately still in bondage, still not free, still not able to share in that rallying cry so often found in Mrs. Lessing's fiction. At one point, in his delirium, Watkins conceives of a "broth of microbes" taking on intelligence and will, vaguely akin to Raskolnikov's similar vision in the epilogue to *Crime and Punishment;* for Watkins, though, this is merely one of many ways of seeing a terrible cleavage in man, between his sense of community and his sense of individuality. Harmony, we are told (in the celestial gathering mentioned above), is the only way in which the creatures on Earth can prosper. But instead of Harmony, human aggression, irrationality, and irresponsibility increase, still strands in a single operation called Life.

Dealing as it does with a kind of schizophrenia, this novel is especially indebted to the writings of the noted British psychiatrist, R. D. Laing. Many parallels between *Briefing* and Laing's work can be found, but the parallel between a chapter of his *The Politics of Experience* entitled "A Ten-Day Voyage" is especially fruitful.[4] Not only does Laing discuss "inner space" as does Lessing, he also provides a list of "directions" a schizoid person can follow in his road to recovery and, even more, does this with a character surnamed Watkins. First noted, so far as I can detect, by Lois Marchino,[5] this correspondence develops through a trip taken by a schizophrenic experiencing hallucinations of strange animals, he envisions "gods," and he eventually decides to come back to "normality." Laing's statement here is valuable: "Can we not see that *this voyage is not what we need to be cured of, but that it is itself a natural way of healing our own appalling state of alienation called normality?*"[6] Much clearly needs to be done yet with this relatively late development in Lessing's thought; certainly, those working with Laing will be especially well provided with source material.

The Four-Gated City ended, as we have noted, with a terrible apocalyptic vision suggesting the end of civilization and human life. In *Briefing,* an apocalyptic sense is also to be found, but more in emotional and mental terms than in social or physical. For Watkins has gone through a deterioration of psychic equilibrium tantamount to a "dark night of the soul" or "descent into hell" with no certain glittering outcome or bright breakthrough of light. That he does become restored to "normality" is less a tribute to man's knowledge of psychic processes than to the potentially de- bilitating effects of electric-shock therapy. In a brief after- word, Mrs. Lessing comments on knowing intimately a person who "experiences everything differently from 'nor- mal' people," and adds that the point (referring specifically to a film on which she was working) was that the hero's "extra sensitivity and perception must be a handicap in a society organized as ours is, to favour the conforming, the average, the obedient." But even the therapists themselves, foremost in their profession, do not agree among them- selves as to either the means of therapy or the causes of psy- chic imbalance. She comments that education, as we know it today, consists of putting labels on things, to categorize neatly, to see all of existence, in a word, as neatly fitting predetermined pigeonholes, instead of allowing for individ- ual perceptions and awarenesses and experiences. As in *The Four-Gated City*, the suggestion is made that these non- conforming perceptions may indeed be more real even than the conventionally predictable and safe alternatives a con- formist society advocates and praises.

Rather than her creative powers seeming to diminish in this most recent work, Mrs. Lessing seems intent on prob- ing more and more deeply and relentlessly into the inner- most recesses of human experience, to move away from the political and social novels of two decades ago into a virtually unexplored territory, into profound explorations of the areas of human experience that ultimately are the most dif- ficult to handle—especially in a creative effort such as a novel—and to dismiss lightly. As noted before, though, this book differs in several significant ways from her previous efforts, not the least in its presenting a male protagonist instead of the kind of woman easy to generalize about in her other novels. Indeed, even a cursory examination of the lives and characteristics of her several major female pro- tagonists will suggest considerable similarity, so much so, in fact, that one is rather accurate if he refers to all these women as reflecting one archetypal or prototypal woman that Mrs. Lessing seems obsessed with.

This woman is invariably self-consciously aware of her "emancipated" status: in a masculine world, she attempts to establish an identity uniquely her own. In the process of doing this, she deliberately seeks out the areas of life that she has either not known or had available to her previously, or that had been considered unseemly for her to know. She is initiated sexually, for instance, but despite a greater and greater degree of sexual experience, she is rarely satisfied; only in those rare circumstances when she feels she is accepted as a person and for herself, with this relationship culminating in love, does she find it possible to achieve orgasm. Politically she is also inexperienced at first, but, being basically idealistic, she attempts, through involvement with militantly radical groups such as the Communist party, to carry out those ideals into practice. When political disillusionment sets in, as it inevitably and invariably does, she leaves the party for some more effective way of serving humanity. The racial struggle, especially that in British colonial Africa, fills her with the kind of righteous indignation which cries out for immediate alleviation of the injustices. A sensitive person, she reads widely, and not surprisingly bases much of her expectations about life on that reading. She also dreams regularly, with these dreams, as recorded in the novels, almost always having a contrapuntal or symbolic relationship to her life while awake. She repeatedly shows evidence of wanting to suffer: not only is this suggested by her dreams, but perhaps even more by masochistic tendencies in her behavior. Almost always she chooses for a lover a Jew, and usually a Jew who is self-consciously aware of his status as a pariah in a non-Jewish society. Significantly, even though she espouses radical political and racial movements, not once does she have a romantic or sexual relationship with a nonwhite, even in those novels set in such a relatively open society as England. And, perhaps most significant of all the parallels between the women in these novels, she is constantly willing to turn her back on a previous way of life and to accept eagerly the promise of the new.

The foregoing suggests that Mrs. Lessing frequently tells

and retells the same story about the same person, even, as one critic suggests, with similar names repeatedly chosen for the characters: Myra, Molly, Millie, Martha, and so forth.[7] But this is not mere lack of imagination or ability to create significant plot. Rather, these several novels, concerned as they are with the same essential situations, comprise variations on the themes mentioned above, race, politics, sex, and so on. Repeating in this manner is not in itself unheard of among writers; one might single out, among American writers, Hemingway and Faulkner for doing much the same thing, the former with his variations on heroism and the latter with his variations on the sickness and decline of a particular section of our country. The critic cited above suggests that Mrs. Lessing, as a moralist, "comes back always to the same questions and tests them against her own experience."[8] Hence Mrs. Lessing's fiction is an effort to examine from several distinct perspectives attitudes toward each of the subjects with which she is most greatly and directly concerned, and by that means to effect the same search suggested by Martha Quest's surname: the search for truth about existence, especially the existence of a person like her prototypal heroine.

Given the premises in the foregoing paragraph, one can perhaps see the curious relationship Mrs. Lessing has to modern fiction in general. Rarely, for instance, does she venture forth with technical innovations such as those identified with Joyce; only in The Golden Notebook and the Four-Gated City does she attempt anything radical in form, and she considers her effort in the former novel to be a failure, especially since most reviewers misunderstood her intentions;[9] in the "Free Women" sections of that novel (themselves comprising a short novel) and in most of her other works, she is conventionally concerned with a purely expository, chronological narration of the events in the lives of her characters. It was mentioned above that several of her novels have a conventionally Victorian opening; one might say the same about the endings, for in several of the books —notably excepting The Grass Is Singing, of course, and the Four-Gated City—the protagonist leaves the comfortable existence she has enjoyed for the uncertainties of the future. Superficially, this leaving may be compared to that of Ibsen's Nora in *A Doll's House,* but Mrs. Lessing's heroines have a substantiality and a toughness about them unlike the subjects of nineteenth-century fiction or drama. The *Children of Violence* series in particular has appeared to different readers as being essentially a Victorian novel.[10] Hence the technical considerations, again in common with "intuitive" writers such as D. H. Lawrence, are subordinated to the thematic:

> No one will read Doris Lessing in order to learn how to write a good novel or in order to admire a beautiful work of art. She disdains—is suspicious of—smoothness of most sorts. There is nothing subtle about her fiction; its bulk alone is formidable. She is careless even about sentences; she overwrites; her "symbolism" tends to be self-conscious; she preaches when she should be demonstrating; she tells us too much and too often. But frankly I don't care. More than anyone else writing today, Doris Lessing speaks to the question that the young Martha Quest asks of the novels she reads: "What does this say about my life?" If we are not Nora, if we have not slammed a door, we live with or next to someone who has. This is why women (and men in self-defense) are reading Doris Lessing.[11]

Such considerations as style are somewhat outside my concern, but the answer to the question raised by Martha and quoted in this statement is, as has been suggested in each of the earlier chapters, commitment. But this does not imply mere "slamming of a door" in the typically feminist manner; Mrs. Lessing, as we have indicated, is concerned with the *quality* of commitment, not its mere existence, for an imbalance of commitments leads to the psychic destruction of the individual, somewhat as presented in *Briefing for a Descent into Hell.*

Mrs. Lessing has described this necessary balance of commitments, without using these exact words, in the essay in which her fictional "credo" was set forth. After saying that she was looking in the great nineteenth-century novels for the "warmth, the compassion, the humanity, the love of people" found in those books but lacking in today's, she says:

> This is what I mean when I say that literature should be committed. It is these qualities which I demand, and which I believe spring from being committed; for one cannot be committed without belief.
>
> Committed to what? Not to being a propagandist for any political party. I never have thought so. I see no reason why writers should not work, in their role as citizens, for a political party; but they should never allow themselves to feel obliged to publicize any party policy or "line" unless their own private passionate need as writers makes them do so: in which case the passion might, if they have talent enough, make literature of the propaganda.
>
> Once a writer has a feeling of responsibility, as a human being, for the other human beings he influences, it seems to me he must become a humanist, and must feel himself as an instrument of change for good or for bad. That image of the pretty singer in the ivory tower has always seemed to be a dishonest one. Logically he should be content to sing to his image in the mirror. The act of getting a story or a novel published is an act of communication, an attempt to impose one's personality and beliefs on other people. If a writer accepts this responsibility, he must see himself, to use the socialist phrase, as an architect of the soul, and it is a phrase which none of the old nineteenth-century novelists would have shied away from.[12]

Following this statement, Mrs. Lessing indicates that a "vision to build toward" must be held by the individual if he is to be such an "architect." That is, it is not enough to have a commitment, regardless of its source or reason for continuing to hold it; one must go beyond the mere fact of being committed to, say, communism, to an understanding of man and the world in which he lives.

Certainly the majority of the central characters discussed have one or another kind of commitment; but one wonders not only if each such character knows why he has that commitment, but also if he knows what is implied for his and others' lives in having it. Mere commitment by itself thus becomes in effect no more than the bureaucracy and conformity so often attacked in these novels by Mrs. Lessing, and is not in itself a viable way of life. Again, Mrs. Lessing has stated the choice tersely in her essay:

> There are only two choices: that we force ourselves into the effort of imagination necessary to become what we are capable of being; or that we submit to being ruled by the office boys of big business, or the socialist bureacrats [sic] who have forgotten that socialism means a desire for goodness and compassion—and the end of submission is that we shall blow ourselves up.[13]

Now, most of Mrs. Lessing's heroines believe that being committed to a life free of bureaucracy and conformity necessarily leads to a self-consciously "emancipated" or "free" status in society. But this is self-delusion: Mrs. Lessing has said that she doesn't see herself as a "free woman," "only because I don't think anyone is 'free.' "[14] She has also claimed that she doesn't understand the word "freedom" and could give neither a rational nor an irrational defense of it:

> On the contrary, it seems to me that every human being is unfree from the moment of conception, since he is a chance conglomeration of inherited things, his parents' attitudes, the people who chance to influence him, wars, national attitudes and so on. Who am I? Who are you?[15]

The best illustrations to support this obviously naturalistic statement of Mrs. Lessing's are Martha Quest's daughter, whom Martha believes she is "setting free," but who in reality is thoroughly influenced by Mrs. Quest and the conformist society of Douglas and the child's stepmother; and Anna Wulf, who finds that writing a novel about ostensibly "free" women is a means of achieving sanity.

This matter of "freedom" is considerably less clear and ambiguous than Mrs. Lessing doubtlessly intended; another of today's women writers from England, Storm Jameson, for example, has commented about allegedly "pornographic" novels, clearly referring to *The Golden Notebook*, in this fashion:

Is it, perhaps, the latest stage in becoming a "free woman," allowed or compelled to live a free life, the freest conceivable this side of anarchy? This would seem plausible except that in the most intelligent novel of this kind I have read these anxiously free women are caught in their sexuality like flies in treacle. Sexual emotion is far and away the most complex of human impulses: hunger, ambition, parenthood, the controlled ferocities of artist and scientist can at any time, in any man or woman, elbow it aside: none of them equals it in depth and range of force. But if a serious artist is moved to recite the physical details of the sexual act, the degree of his success is measurable by his readers' sense of their point and moment as part of the bodily and spiritual disturbance touched off by the erotic impulse itself, going far beyond the act. To offer them as of interest in themselves to an adult reader is a form of exhibitionism, a nervous tic, rather than a creative impulse of the writer in control of himself. And, indeed, exhibitionism is the only word strictly descriptive of any novel I have come across by an English (or American) woman writer in which an obvious effort has been made to write, as its author might say, frankly and fearlessly about sexual behaviour—including the involuntary aspects of female sexuality.[16]

But the ironies of the term "free women," as has been suggested, are such as to make it perfectly clear that even if such women are free of marriage, they are still bound in other ways, especially bound to their biological natures and drives:

Hence, the "free" woman is free only in a most limited sense. She is free to choose between her divided selves:

free to attempt the "precarious balance" of living with both of them; free to be "female" or to be a "free woman." Finally, free comes to mean divided. The free woman divided, in Mrs. Lessing's novels, suffers most from a feeling of failure.[17]

One is free, therefore, only when, as with Anna in the "Free Women" sections of *The Golden Notebook*, one discards the obsessive concern with commitments of an earlier day and dedicates oneself to humanity, to individuals. As all of Mrs. Lessing's protagonists discover, fiction—both reading and writing fiction—is one of the key ways of noting this dedication, for the novel, Mrs. Lessing believes, is uniquely available as a means by which one individual can speak with another individual. The novelist's "small personal voice," then, is the only way in which the essence of what it is to be human, the "warmth and humanity and love of people," can be experienced in the complex, chaotic, conformist world in which we live.[18]

Notes

1 – Doris Lessing in Perspective

1. Irving Howe, "Neither Compromise Nor Happiness," *New Republic*, 15 December 1962, p. 17.

2. Jeremy Brooks, "Doris Lessing's Chinese Box," *Sunday Times* (London), 15 April 1962.

3. Among those recent studies of the modern novel either mentioning Mrs. Lessing only in passing or devoting an insignificant amount of attention to her are Walter Allen, *The Modern Novel in Britain and the United States* (New York: E. P. Dutton, 1964), which devotes slightly more than a page to her, and Frederick Karl, *A Reader's Guide to the Contemporary English Novel* (Farrar, Straus, and Cudahy, 1962), which devotes two pages. See bibliography for other references to recent criticism.

4. "Doris Lessing: The Free Woman's Commitment," in *Contemporary British Novelists*, ed. Charles Shapiro (Carbondale: Southern Illinois University Press, 1965), pp. 48–61.

5. Some of the more significant essays and books concerned with Mrs. Lessing's work are cited in the bibliography. Ironically, the dearth of critical studies—and doctoral dissertations —devoted to this work that lasted until, say, 1970 (my own dissertation [Southern Illinois University, 1968] was the second written on Lessing) now seems threatened to be supplanted by an avalanche of more and more ingenious and subtle analyses. The first annual seminar on Lessing was held at the Modern Language Association's 1971 convention in Chicago, at which time at least a dozen dissertations-in-progress were noted.

6. The major biographical sources are Doris Lessing, "All Seething Underneath," *Vogue*, 143 (15 February 1964), 80–81, 132–33; "Myself as Sportsman," *New Yorker*, 31 (21 June

1963), 93–96; "The Small Personal Voice," in *Declaration*, ed. Tom Maschler (London: MacGibbon and Kee, 1957), pp. 11–27; an interview with Mrs. Lessing in *Counterpoint*, ed. Roy Newquist (Chicago: Rand McNally, 1964), pp. 413–24; a brief "portrait" in *Publisher's Weekly*, 161 (2 February 1952), 706; Thomas Wiseman, "Mrs. Lessing's Kind of Life," *Time and Tide*, 42 (12 April 1962), 26–29; and brief summaries in such reference works as *Who's Who*, vol. 113 (London: A. and C. Black, 1961) and *Contemporary Authors*, vol. 9–10 (Detroit: Gale Research Co., 1964).

7. Much of the information in this paragraph is paraphrased from Neal Wood, *Communism and British Intellectuals* (New York: Columbia University Press, 1959), esp. pp. 57–63 and 198–202.

8. Dorothy Brewster, *Doris Lessing* (New York: Twayne Publishers, 1965), p. 167.

2 – The Grass Is Singing

1. Information taken from the jacket of the English edition (Michael Joseph, 1950); all page numbers, given parenthetically, refer to this edition.

2. "Being Prohibited," *New Statesman*, 21 April 1956, pp. 410–12. For a detailed discussion of the trip itself, dedicated to "good friends, both in London and Central Africa, white and black, who helped me during my trip, and while writing the book, with time, money, experience and advice," see her *Going Home* (London: Michael Joseph, 1957), from which edition quotations are taken. The only American edition was issued in paperback by Ballantine Books in 1968.

3. Interview with Doris Lessing in *Counterpoint*, ed. Roy Newquist (Chicago: Rand McNally, 1964), p. 422.

4. Lessing, *Going Home*, p. 19.

5. Ibid.

6. Ibid.

7. Ibid, p. 95.

8. Ibid., pp. 24–25.

9. R. P. Draper, *D. H. Lawrence*, English Authors Series (New York: Twayne Publishers, 1964), pp. 172–73. The reference to Moses' washing himself occurs in the novel on pp. 176–78.

10. Dorothy Brewster, *Doris Lessing* (New York: Twayne Publishers, 1965), 158–61.

11. D. H. Lawrence, *Women in Love*, Compass Books ed. (New York: Viking Press, 1960). Relevant passages are from pp. 67 and 245–46; also cf. pp. 32, 71–72, and 87.

12. Draper, *Lawrence*, p. 172.

13. Brewster, *Lessing*, p. 40.

14. Interview with Doris Lessing in *Counterpoint*, p. 415.

15. Personal letter to Alfred A. Carey, 10 March 1965.

16. In my earlier essay, "Doris Lessing: The Free Woman's Commitment," *Contemporary British Novelists*, ed. Charles Shapiro (Carbondale: Southern Illinois University Press, 1965), I imply that Mary Turner is like Mrs. Lessing's other "free" women. But a letter from Mrs. Lessing correctly points out that such is not the case:

> I'm rather surprised to see that you see Mary Turner as like other of my characters. Where, at any point in that novel does she feel any concern for the African servants or their treatment: On the contrary, she is so much a product of that society it never crosses her mind to think on those lines. [Letter from Doris Lessing to Paul Schlueter, 24 June 1965]

3 – *The* Children of Violence Series

1. Doris Lessing, "The Small Personal Voice," in *Declaration*, ed. Tom Maschler (London: MacGibbon and Kee, 1957), p. 22.

2. The titles and publication dates of the five individual volumes are as follows: *Martha Quest*, 1952; *A Proper Marriage*, 1954; *A Ripple from the Storm*, 1958; *Landlocked*, 1965; and *The Four-Gated City*, 1969. The first two were published in the United States in one volume entitled *Children of Violence* by Simon and Schuster in 1964, and the second two in one volume with the same title by Simon and Schuster in 1966; the final volume was published by Alfred A. Knopf. All page references (henceforth given parenthetically) are to these editions, with volume numbers applying respectively to the five parts given before each page reference.

3. The current American reprint of this influential book includes a perceptive appreciative essay by Mrs. Lessing (Greenwich, Conn.: Fawcett Publications, 1968).

4. D. H. Lawrence, *Women in Love*, Compass Books ed. (New York: Viking Press, 1960), p. 156.

5. Ibid., p. 159.

6. Paul Barker, "Doris Lessing: The Uses of Repetition," *New Society,* 24 June 1965, pp. 27–28.

7. The observation about the initial sentences of some of Mrs. Lessing's novels was first suggested by Lawrence Graver in his review of volumes 3 and 4 of the series, "The Commonplace Book of Doris Lessing," *New Republic,* 2 April 1966, p. 27.

8. Interview with Joseph Haas, *Panorama, Chicago Daily News,* 14 June 1969, pp. 4–5.

9. Ibid.

10. Frederick P. W. McDowell, "Recent British Fiction: Some Established Writers," *Contemporary Literature* 2 No. 3 (Summer 1970), pp. 427–28.

4 – The Golden Notebook

1. *Each His Own Wilderness,* in *New English Dramatists,* ed. E. Martin Browne (Harmondsworth, Middlesex: Penguin Books, 1959), p. 41.

2. Ibid., p. 50.

3. Toward the end of Anna's delirious descent into nightmare, she dreams of a tiger crouched to attack her. Unlike her other nightmares, though, Anna is able in this one to fight back and to realize that she has nothing to fear from the tiger. Half awake after this realization, Anna decides to write a play about herself, Saul, and the tiger (pp. 525–27).

4. For an intelligent brief discussion of Mrs. Lessing's several plays and their relationship to the works of other contemporary British playwrights, see John Russell Taylor, *Anger and After* (Baltimore: Penguin Books, 1963), pp. 195–96.

5. "Footnote to *The Golden Notebook,*" interview with Doris Lessing by Robert Rubens, *Queen,* 21 August 1962, p. 31.

6. Interview in *Counterpoint,* ed. Roy Newquist (Chicago: Rand McNally, 1964), p. 418.

7. Personal letter from Doris Lessing to Paul Schlueter, 24 July 1965.

8. The points and quotations in this paragraph are summarized from the interview with Mrs. Lessing in the *Queen,* p. 31.

9. Ibid., p. 32.

10. Ibid.; italics are Mrs. Lessing's.

11. Personal letter from Doris Lessing to Paul Schlueter, 24 July 1965.

12. "Footnote to *The Golden Notebook*," *Queen*, p. 32.

13. Interview in *Counterpoint*, p. 418.

14. Doris Lessing, *The Golden Notebook* (New York: Simon and Schuster, 1962), p. 568. (Since the three most common editions of *The Golden Notebook* currently available in English [the British edition, published in London by Michael Joseph in 1962, the Simon and Schuster edition, 1962, and the first American paperback edition, published in New York by McGraw-Hill in 1963] are photographic facsimiles and have exactly the same pagination, references can apply to any of the three. Page references will hereafter be inserted parenthetically following quotations or allusions.) The first published reference to this seeming discrepancy of endings, incidentally, appeared in Granville Hicks's review of the novel, *Saturday Review*, 30 June 1962, p. 16. Since the McGraw-Hill paperback was issued, the novel has also been issued by Ballantine in a mass-circulation reprint edition.

15. Quoted in *Counterpoint*, p. 422.

16. The best brief, recent discussion of the background and subsequent history of Rhodesia is Patrick Keatley, *The Politics of Partnership* (Baltimore: Penguin Books, 1962).

17. But on p. 83 we are informed that there were no black trade unions.

18. "The Small Personal Voice," in *Declaration*, ed. Tom Maschler (London: MacGibbon and Kee, 1957), p. 26.

19. Ibid., p. 20.

20. Personal letter from Doris Lessing to Alfred A. Carey, 10 March 1965.

21. Personal letter from Doris Lessing to Paul Schlueter, 24 July 1965.

22. "The Small Personal Voice," *Declaration*, p. 17.

23. Mrs. Marks is evidently a Jungian therapist, although this is not specified; psychoanalysts in England need not be physicians.

24. "The Small Personal Voice," *Declaration*, p. 27.

25. Ibid., p. 16.

26. Ibid.

27. Interview in *Counterpoint*, p. 418.

28. "The Small Personal Voice," *Declaration*, p. 14.

29. Ibid., p. 16.

30. Ibid., p. 20.

5–Retreat to Innocence *and* Briefing for a Descent into Hell

1. The only American edition, now out-of-print, was published in a Prometheus paperback edition in 1959 by Marzani and Munzell (New York); this edition is a photographic copy of the British edition published in 1956 by Michael Joseph, so page references (given parenthetically) can apply to either edition.

2. Dorothy Brewster quotes Mrs. Lessing as feeling that the characters, especially the two central characters, Julia and Jan, "were wasted, because their possibilities were not fully developed" *Doris Lessing* (New York: Twayne Publishers, 1965), p. 103. In correspondence, Mrs. Lessing has said essentially the same thing: it is a "good theme spoiled by lack of thought. Good material wasted, I see that novel as" (personal letter to Paul Schlueter, 24 July 1965), and "The reason why I don't like *Retreat* is because I think a good many very serious questions were far too easily, lightly, treated. I'd like the book to get lost altogether. Not that some of the scenes and characters aren't all right. But it is a soft book" (personal letter to Alfred A. Carey, 10 March 1965).

3. Alfred A. Knopf, 1971.

4. R. D. Laing, *The Politics of Experience and The Bird of Paradise* (Harmondsworth: Penguin Books, 1968), pp. 120–37. For useful interpretive studies of Laing, see James S. Gordon, "Who Is Mad? Who Is Sane?," *Atlantic*, January 1971, pp. 50–66; and Peter Mezan, "After Freud and Jung, Now Comes R. D. Laing," *Esquire*, January 1972, pp. 92–97, 160–78.

5. Lois Marchino, "The Search for Self in the Novels of Doris Lessing," *The Fiction of Doris Lessing: Papers Collected for MLA Seminar 46*, 1971.

6. Laing, *Politics of Experience*, p. 136; italics in original.

7. Paul Barker, "Doris Lessing: The Uses of Repetition," *New Society*, 24 June 1965, pp. 27–28.

8. Ibid., p. 28.

9. Florence Howe, "A Talk With Doris Lessing," *Nation*, 6 March 1967, pp. 312–13.

10. See, e.g., Florence Howe, "Doris Lessing's Free Women," *Nation*, 11 January 1965, p. 34.

11. Ibid., p. 37.

12. "The Small Personal Voice," in *Declaration*, ed. Tom Maschler (London: MacGibbon and Kee, 1957), pp. 15–16.

13. Ibid., p. 17.

14. Personal letter from Doris Lessing to Paul Schlueter, 24 July 1965.

15. Personal letter from Doris Lessing to Alfred A. Carey, 10 March 1965.

16. Storm Jameson, "Love's Labours Exposed," *Spectator*, no. 7180, 4 February 1966, p. 134.

17. Howe, "Doris Lessing's Free Women," p. 34.

18. "The Small Personal Voice," *Declaration*, p. 27.

Selected Bibliography

Articles, Interviews, and Letters by Doris Lessing

"Afterword" to Olive Schreiner, *The Story of an African Farm*. Greenwich, Conn.: Fawcett Publications, Inc. 1968, pp. 273–90.

"All Seething Underneath." *Vogue*, 15 February 1964, pp. 80–81, 132–33.

"Being Prohibited." *New Statesman*, 21 April 1956, pp. 410–12.

"Crisis in Central Africa: The Fruits of Humbug." *Twentieth Century*, 165 (April 1959), 368–76.

"Footnote to *The Golden Notebook*." Interview with Robert Rubens, *Queen*, 21 August 1962, pp. 30–32.

Interview with Joseph Haas. *Panorama, Chicago Daily News*, 14 June 1969, pp. 4–5.

Interview with Roy Newquist, *Counterpoint*, ed. Roy Newquist. Chicago: Rand McNally, 1964, pp. 414–25.

"Kariba Project." *New Statesman*, 9 June 1956, pp. 647–48.

"Letter to the Editor." *New Statesman*, 3 November 1961, p. 651.

"London Diary." *New Statesman*, 15, 22 March 1958, pp. 326–27, 367–68.

"Myself As Sportsman." *New Yorker*, 21 June 1963, pp. 92–96.

"Ordinary People." *New Statesman*, 25 June 1960, p. 932.

Personal letter to Alfred A. Carey, 10 March 1965.

Personal letter to Paul Schlueter, 24 July 1965.

"Smart Set Socialists." *New Statesman*, 1 December 1961, pp. 822–24.

"The Small Personal Voice." In *Declaration*, ed. Tom Maschler. London: MacGibbon and Kee, 1957, pp. 11–27.

"A Talk with Doris Lessing." Interview with Florence Howe. *Nation*, 6 March 1967, pp. 311–13.

"What Really Matters." *Twentieth Century*, 172 (Autumn 1963), 96–98.

"Zambia's Joyful Week." *New Statesman*, 6 November 1964, pp. 692, 694.

Books or Articles All or Partly about Doris Lessing and Her Background

Allen, Walter. *The Modern Novel in Britain and the United States*. New York: E. P. Dutton, 1965, pp. 197, 276–77.

Brewster, Dorothy. *Doris Lessing*, English Authors Series. New York: Twayne Publishers, 1965.

Burgess, Anthony. *The Novel Now: A Guide to Contemporary Fiction*. New York: W. W. Norton, 1967, pp. 99–101, 105, 122, 158.

Burkom, Selma R. "A Doris Lessing Checklist." *Critique*, 11, no. 1 (1969), 69–81.

————. " 'Only Connect': Form and Content in the Works of Doris Lessing." *Critique*, 11, no. 1 (1969), 51–68.

Carey, Alfred A. "Doris Lessing: The Search for Reality." Ph.D. dissertation, University of Wisconsin, 1965.

Churchill, Caryl. "Not Ordinary, Not Safe." *Twentieth Century*, 167 (November 1960), 443–51.

Draper, R. P. *D. H. Lawrence*, English Authors Series. New York: Twayne Publishers, 1964, pp. 172–73.

"The Fog of Ways." *TLS*, 27 April 1962, pp. 280.

Gindin, James. *Postwar British Fiction*. Berkeley: University of California Press, 1962, pp. 65–86.

Howe, Florence. "Doris Lessing's Free Women." *Nation*, 11 January 1965, pp. 34–37.

Jameson, Storm. "Love's Labours Exposed." *Spectator*, no. 7180 (4 February 1966), p. 134.

Karl, Frederick. *A Reader's Guide to the Contemporary British Novel*. New York: Farrar, Straus, and Cudahy, 1962, pp. 281–83.

Keatley, Patrick. *The Politics of Partnership*. Baltimore: Penguin Books, 1962.

McDowell, Frederick P. W. "The Devious Involutions of Human Character and Emotions: Reflections on Some Recent British Novels." *Wisconsin Studies in Contemporary Literature*, 4 (Autumn 1963), 339–66.

————. "The Fiction of Doris Lessing: An Interim View." *Arizona Quarterly*, 21, no. 4 (Winter 1965), 215–45.

————. "Recent British Fiction: Some Established Winters," *Contemporary Literature*, 11, no. 3 (Summer 1970), pp. 424–28.

Morris, Robert. *Continuance and Change: The Contemporary British Novel Sequence*. Carbondale: Southern Illinois University Press, 1972, pp. 1–27.

Rabinovitz, Rubin. *The Reaction Against Experiment in the English Novel, 1950–1960*. New York: Columbia University Press, 1967, pp. 14–15, 29–30, 78, 86, 167.

Schlueter, Paul. "Doris Lessing: The Free Woman's Commitment," in *Contemporary British Novelists*, ed. Charles Shapiro. Carbondale: Southern Illinois University Press, 1965, pp. 48–61.

Taylor, John Russell, *Anger and After*. Baltimore: Penguin Books, 1963, pp. 195–96.

Tucker, Martin. *Africa in Modern Literature* (New York: Ungar, 1967), pp. 175–83.

Wellwarth, George. *The Theatre of Protest and Paradox: Developments in the Avant-Garde Drama*. New York: New York University Press, 1964, pp. 197, 248–50.

Wiseman, Thomas. "Mrs. Lessing's Kind of Life." *Time and Tide*, 43 (12 April 1962), 264.

Wood, Neal. *Communism and British Intellectuals*. New York: Columbia University Press, 1959.

Selected Critical Reviews

Barker, Paul. "Doris Lessing: The Uses of Repetition." *New Society*, 24 June 1965, pp. 27–28. (Review of *Landlocked*.)

Bergonzi, Bernard. "In Pursuit of Doris Lessing." *New York Review of Books*, 11 February 1965, pp. 12–14. (Review of *Children of Violence*, vols. 1 and 2.)

Bliven, Naomi. "It's Not a Woman's World." *New Yorker*, 1 June 1963, pp. 114–19. (Review of *The Golden Notebook*.)

Dienstag, Eleanor. "The Self-Analysis of Doris Lessing." *New Republic*, 9 January 1965, pp. 19–20. (Review of *Children of Violence*, vols. 1 and 2.)

Graver, Lawrence. "The Commonplace Book of Doris Lessing." *New Republic*, 2 April 1966, pp. 27–29. (Review of *Children of Violence*, vols. 3 and 4.)

Hicks, Granville. "All About a Modern Eve." *Saturday Review*,

2 April 1966, pp. 31–32. (Review of *Children of Violence*, vols. 3 and 4, and Dorothy Brewster, *Doris Lessing*.)

—————. "Complexities of a Free Woman." *Saturday Review*, 30 June 1962, p. 16. (Review of *The Golden Notebook*.)

Howe, Florence. "Doris Lessing: Child of Violence." *The Nation*, 13 June 1966, pp. 716–18. (Review of *Children of Violence*, vols. 3 and 4.)

Howe, Irving. "Neither Compromise nor Happiness." *New Republic*, 15 December 1962, pp. 17–20. (Review of *The Golden Notebook*.)

Nott, Kathleen. "Counterpoint to Lawrence." *Time and Tide*, 43, 26 April 1962, p. 30. (Review of *The Golden Notebook*.)

Schlueter, Paul. "Enduring Chronicle of Martha Quest." *Panorama, Chicago Daily News*, 2 April 1966, p. 7. (Review of *Children of Violence*, vols. 3 and 4.)

—————. "A Chilling Novel of Destruction and Survival." *Panorama, Chicago Daily News*, 14 June 1969, pp. 4–5. (Review of *The Four-Gated City*.)

Taubman, Robert. "Near Zero." *New Statesman*, 8 November 1963, pp. 653–54. (Review of *The Golden Notebook*.)

Index

143